Sugar-Free Cooking With

STEVIA

The Naturally Sweet & Calorie-Free Herb

FOURTH EDITION, REVISED

James & Tanya Kirkland

FOREWORD BY
DR. H.J. ROBERTS, M.D. F.A.C.P.

Crystal Health Publishing
Arlington, Texas

Published by:

Crystal Health Publishing
PO Box 171683
Arlington, TX 76003-1683
United States

Disclaimer: This book is written for informational purposes only. It is not intended to diagnose or prescribe for any medical condition nor to replace common sense and reasonable caution in consuming stevia products. If you have any health concerns such as diabetes, cancer, or pregnancy, consult your physician before beginning any new diet or exercise regime. This book should not be used as a substitute for your physician's advice. Neither the authors nor the publisher is responsible for defects in the manufacturing, processing or handling of stevia products. Although the authors and publisher have exhaustively researched all sources to ensure the accuracy of the information contained in this book, we assume no responsibility for errors, inaccuracies, omissions or any other inconsistency herein.

Copyright © 1998, 1999, 2000, 2002
First Printing 1998
Second Printing 1998
Third Printing 1999, 2nd Edition, completely revised
Fourth Printing 2000, 3rd Edition, Revised
Fifth Printing 2002, 3rd Edition, Revised
Printed in the United States of America

Library of Congress Catalog Card Number: 99-98115

Library of Congress Cataloging-in-Publication Data
(Provided by Quality Books, Inc.)
Kirkland, James, 1965-
Sugar-free cooking with stevia : the naturally sweet & calorie free herb / James & Tanya Kirkland. - 3rd ed.
p. cm.
    Includes bibliographical references and index.
    ISBN 1-928906-15-X
1. Cookery (Stevia)
2. Stevia Rebaudiana.
3. Sugar-free diet-Recipes. I. Kirkland, Tanya. II. Title.
TX 819.s757 2000   641.5'635   QB199-1890

Sugar-Free Cooking With
STEVIA

We dedicate this book to our daughters,
Tatiana and Sophia.
May your lives always be sweet!

Table of Contents

Appendix

Foreword

BY H.J. ROBERTS, M.D., F.A.C.P.

I have been concerned about the undesirable effects of both sugar and aspartame. They extend as far back as four decades in the case of sugar. Such concern stems from clinical observations in the trenches of a medical practice as an internist/endocrinologist/consultant. It has been reinforced by scores of my published corporate-neutral researches. They are listed for interested readers.

The magnitude of sugar and aspartame consumption is staggering. Indeed, I have come to the conclusion that it poses a profound public health menace. This may be difficult for many consumers to appreciate because of the widespread hype they encounter, coupled with health professionals influenced by flawed studies and misleading interpretations.

In the case of aspartame products, my data on more than 1300 persons afflicted with Aspartame Disease – a term I coined – seem to justify my repeated recommendation that they be removed from the market as an "imminent public health hazard." This reflects their multiple neurotoxic, metabolic, allergenic, and fetal/carcinogenic effects . . . as explained in my publications and position papers. Those at high risk include persons with diabetes, hypoglycemia, migraine, epilepsy, visual problems, depression, memory loss, eating disorders, and pregnant women, as well as infants and children.

These comments are not scare tactics by an alleged "media terrorist." Rather, they represent a sense of responsibility by an independent and objective physician/scientist, and a concerned citizen.

It is in this context that the introduction of an acceptable sugar substitute, which appears to be safe based on extended use throughout the world, should be welcomed. Accordingly, James and Tanya Kirkland deserve praise for their persistent efforts in developing and revising Sugar-Free Cooking With Stevia.

Introduction

As Americans, we love our sweets, but we know now that refined sugar can give us more health trouble than it's worth. We don't want to give up our treats, but we also want to feel healthy, so what can we do? In late 1988 the answer virtually fell into my lap. I encountered stevia, an herb 15 times sweeter than sugar that has no sugar and no calories.

Then, stevia only came in dried, whole leaf or powdered form and had a limited number of uses. Also, whole leaf stevia often has a slight licorice flavor - a real turnoff for me. I found the whole leaf forms difficult and inconvenient to use since they did not dissolve in liquid, so I continued consuming foods and beverages full of sugar and (worse) artificial sweeteners.

Almost ten years later, wiser and a bit heavier, I investigated stevia again. This was when I heard about Stevioside, the molecule that makes the stevia leaves sweet (more on this in Chapter 2). Researchers and developers had found new ways to use this 'sweet molecule' to create a variety of stevia products. For example, standardized stevia extract, powder or liquid, can be up to 300 times sweeter than sugar, and a little goes a very long way.

One of the new forms of stevia I found on the market was called a stevia blend or spoonable stevia. This new form combines stevioside extract with the non-sweet filler maltodextrin, which adds bulk and makes it easier to measure. With this easy to manage form, stevia can now replace sugar in most recipes and beverages. I started substituting stevia products for the sugar in my diet and lost 20 pounds. This success inspired me to create the original 'Cooking With Stevia' book. I had no idea it would become a best-selling cookbook, or that it would be temporarily banned by the FDA (see Chapter 4).

Along with the more than 200 kitchen-tested recipes in this book, you will find enlightening and useful information about the stevia herb itself. Our stevia-sweetened recipes are hits with both adults and children, and we hope your family enjoys them as much as ours.

PART ONE

The Sweet Story of Stevia

CHAPTER 1

Frequently Asked Questions

FREQUENTLY ASKED QUESTIONS

1. What is stevia?

2. Is stevia safe?

3. What are the benefits of using stevia?

4. I have Candidiasis; will using stevia help this problem?

5. Is stevia safe to use during pregnancy or when nursing?

6. I've heard that the natives of South America used stevia as a contraceptive. Does stevia reduce fertility?

7. Does stevia have any effect on hypoglycemia or diabetes?

8. Can stevia stop my sugar cravings?

9. Where is stevia grown?

10. What are the types or forms of stevia?

11. Does stevia perform like sugar when used in cooking and baking? Can I substitute stevia for sugar cup for cup?

12. Will stevia lose its sweetness or break down at high temperatures like aspartame?

13. If stevia has been around so long, why am I just now hearing about it?

14. Why are stevia products so expensive?

15. Why aren't diet soft drinks sweetened with stevia?

16. What are the negative effects of aspartame?

17. What should I look for when purchasing Stevioside or stevia blends?

18. What is Maltodextrin?

19. What is F.O.S.?

20. What is Erythritol?

What Everyone Needs to Know about Stevia:

1. What is stevia?

Stevia (pronounced steh-via) is a leafy green plant of the Asteraceae family, genus Stevia, species Rebaudiana. Stevia is related to lettuce, marigold and chicory. You may be familiar with stevia by one of its many other names: Sweet Leaf, Caa-he-È, or Erva Doce. Dr. Moises Santiago Bertoni identified and classified this plant in the late 1800's. He named the plant Stevia Rebaudiani Bertoni in honor of a Paraguayan chemist named Rebaudi. The Guarani Indians in South America had been using the leaves of the plant for centuries to sweeten bitter teas and as a sweet treat. When Dr. Bertoni received samples of the plant, he wrote "one small piece of the leaf will keep the mouth sweet for an hour."

2. Is stevia safe?

Is stevia safe? Absolutely. People have used stevia since pre-Columbian times with no reports of ill effects. Decades of research have proven stevia safe for human and animal consumption, unlike some commercial sweeteners

3. What are the benefits of using stevia?

While the following have not been approved or confirmed by the FDA, studies have shown stevia offers the following benefits:

- Sugarless & adds no calories

- 100% natural, not chemically manufactured

- Potent – 250 to 300 times sweeter than table sugar

- Stable to 392 degrees Fahrenheit (200 degrees Celsius)

- Non-fermentable
- Plaque retardant, anti-caries (prevents cavities)
- Does not impact blood sugar levels
- Non-toxic
- Excellent health safety record

4.I have Candidiasis; will using stevia help this problem?

Candidiasis is a fungal yeast overgrowth in the body that thrives on sugar. Remove sugar and you remove its food source. Stevia will not promote fungal growth as it is a sugar-free natural sweetener.

5. Is stevia safe to use during pregnancy or when nursing?

*When pregnant or nursing, notify your health professional before taking any dietary supplement or drug.

According to recent research and decades of documented stevioside use in Japan, stevioside has no reported negative side effects when used during pregnancy or nursing. In fact, my wife used stevia during all of her pregnancies and while nursing, and our children have been enjoying stevia tea since infancy. They are all bright, healthy and loved.

6. I've heard that the natives of South America used stevia as a contraceptive. Does stevia reduce fertility?

No, stevia does not reduce fertility. There have been reports of native Paraguayan Indians using the whole green stevia leaves for contraceptive purposes. However, according to modern research, steviosides taken orally do not affect fertility.

7. Does stevia have any effect on hypoglycemia or diabetes?

According to scientific research, stevia does not impact blood sugar levels. It allows the body to regulate blood sugar levels naturally. Of course, if you supplement your stevia-sweetened tea with a Twinkie, all bets are off. Fortunately, if you take care with your diet, stevia is a wonderful way to satisfy cravings for sweets without adding sugars. If you suffer from any type of blood sugar condition, always consult with your physician before using any new product.

8. Can stevia stop my sugar cravings?

Many people report that using stevia has helped them reduce or completely eliminate their sugar cravings. These cravings often occur when the blood sugar becomes low. Sugar gives a quick boost of energy that can feel like a brief 'high', followed by a deep crash as the insulin in the pancreas reacts to store the excess sugar in the liver and muscles, thereby lowering blood sugar levels. Eating a balanced diet with enough protein and fat can help eliminate the energy fluctuations that can lead to sugar cravings. Since stevia does not affect blood sugar levels like sugar, it can help break the sugar cycle.

9. Where is stevia grown?

Originally, stevia grew wild in the regions of Northern Paraguay and Southern Brazil. Today, stevia is grown and used around the world. China, Japan, and other Asian countries, South America, Europe, India, the Ukraine and even North America, grow or import stevia and stevia products.

10. What are the types or forms of stevia? (Also, see chapter 2, All Stevias Are NOT Equal)

Stevia Leaves

Fresh Leaves – These have a mild licorice flavor.

Dried Leaves – Dried form of the fresh leaves. Usually about 10-15 times sweeter than sugar. Used in brewing herbal teas and for making liquid extracts.

Tea Cut Leaves – Small pieces that are sifted to remove twigs and other unwanted matter.

Ground Leaves (Powder) – Dried leaves ground into a fine powder. This is used in teas and cooking but does not dissolve.

Liquid Extracts

Dark – A concentrated syrup made from the dried leaves in a base of water and alcohol. Sweetness may vary between manufacturers. This form offers the greatest amount of benefits from the stevia plant.

Clear – A solution of powdered steviosides dissolved in water, alcohol or glycerin. Sweetness varies between manufacturers.

Stevioside Powdered Extracts

'Stevioside' or *'white-powdered stevia'* is the purified or processed form of stevia. Removing unwanted plant matter concentrates the sweet glycosides into an off-white powder 200 to 300 times sweeter than sugar. The quality of the powder depends on the purity of the glycosides (i.e. 80-100% pure). The higher the concentration of stevioside, the better the taste.

Stevia blends

Due to the great strength of the Stevioside Powdered Extracts, manufactures often add filler to "tone" down the strength. This makes the Stevioside easier to use and more palatable. These fillers are usually non-sweet food additives with little to no nutritive value, such as lactose (derived from milk) or maltodextrin. These fillers make the stevia product easier to measure and use in recipes.

11. Does stevia perform like sugar when used in cooking and baking? Can I substitute stevia for sugar cup for cup?

No. The molecular structures of sucrose (sugar) and stevioside differ too much to substitute directly. Sucrose, when heated, will brown or caramelize, making possible such delights as gooey cookies, fudge and caramel. Stevia will not caramelize. In addition, you can not substitute stevia for sugar cup to cup. Because of these differences, cooking with stevia takes some practice. (See Successfully Cooking With Stevia.)

12. Will stevia lose its sweetness or break down at high temperatures like aspartame?

No. One of stevia's biggest advantages is its heat stability. Stevia remains stable to about 392 degrees Fahrenheit, or 200 degrees Celsius, so it can be used in most recipes.

13. If stevia has been around so long, why am I just now learning about it?

Stevia has been around for a long time, even in the United States. Early studies on stevia go back to the 1950's, when the sugar industry fought to prevent the use of stevia in the United States. Greed, corruption and good old-fashioned politics also stood in the way of the public learning about stevia. Today, the manufacturers of chemical sweeteners have lobbied the FDA to prevent stevia's approval as a food additive, even though it has a better health record than any of the chemical sweeteners. If you would like more information, contact "60 Minutes" at CBS. In the Spring of 1997, they aired a report on how the manufacturers of aspartame bought influence with the FDA to push the approval of a sweetener that is now blamed for many illnesses and deaths in America.

14. Why are stevia products so expensive?

Several different factors influence the price of stevia products. As a plant, stevia requires cultivation before it can be harvested for use as a sweetener. This requires large investments of capital to buy plants, farms, equipment, and labor to grow and harvest the plants. Then, there is the expense of processing the leaves into pure stevioside. When compared to sugar and the artificial sweeteners, yes, stevia is expensive; it is not as well-established as the sugar cane industry or as easily produced as the chemical sweeteners. Chemical sweeteners are a blend of inexpensive chemicals that costs very little to manufacture, which is why these companies are so profitable. With more countries growing and processing stevia, prices should soon fall. Also, the newness of stevia to worldwide markets created inefficiencies in delivery and inflated expenses in the supply chain. These should even out as markets become more predictable.

15. Why aren't diet soft drinks sweetened with stevia?

Money, pure and simple. The diet soft drink market is huge, worth billions of dollars, and the manufacturer of aspartame does not want to share that market. Armies of special interest lobbyists were called in to make certain the FDA did not approve stevia for use as a food ingredient. A patent on the aspartame molecule guarantees big profits; stevia is just a natural plant that can be grown by anyone and everyone, and therefore cannot be monopolized.

16. What are the negative effects of aspartame?

Many people chose artificial sweeteners, like aspartame, to replace the sugar in their diet, however, artificial sweeteners have a questionable health record. Aspartame is the number one registered complaint with the FDA, yet it remains approved as a food additive. Aspartame has been linked to several negative effects, including depression of intelligence, loss of short-term memory, gastrointestinal disorders, headaches, visions problems, and seizures.

Ralph G. Walton, MD and Chairman of The Center for Behavioral Medicine and Professor of Clinical Psychiatry, Northeastern Ohio University's College of Medicine, analyzed 164 studies on the health effects of aspartame. Of those 164 cases, 74 had aspartame-related sponsorship and 90 were not funded by the aspartame industry. Of the 90 non-aspartame sponsored studies, 83 (92%) found at least one significant problem with aspartame. Of the 7 studies that found no problems, 6 were conducted by the FDA. Interestingly, several FDA officials involved went to work in the aspartame industry after aspartame was approved as a sweetener.

17. What should I look for when purchasing Stevioside or stevia blends?

For best quality, when purchasing a product with pure steviosides, insist on:

1. A high percentage of steviosides, at least 90%

2. A high percentage of rebaudiosides, at least 20%

3. Unbleached, naturally processed stevioside

4. Organic certification

5. Always buy from a reputable company

18. What is Maltodextrin?

Maltodextrin is a non-sweet complex carbohydrate used as filler in stevia blends, and is virtually tasteless. Maltodextrin can be derived from corn, rice, tapioca, or other starches.

19. What is F.O.S.?

F.O.S. is the common term for fructo-oligosaccharides, which may be blended with Stevioside extract to make 'spoonable stevia'. F.O.S. are naturally occurring sugars, and mildly sweet tasting. F.O.S. promote the growth of certain beneficial internal bacteria. Some people do not tolerate F.O.S. well. These people may experience gas, bloating, or nausea from the use of this product.

20. What is Erythritol?

Although relatively new in the USA, erythritol has been the stevia filler of choice in Japan for years. This white granulated powder is derived from natural grains and fruits. It has virtually no calories and a very low glycemic index. Erythritol has the appearance and texture of white table sugar. Best of all, when combined with a high quality stevioside the resulting stevia blend dissolves quickly and tastes almost like sugar. In addition to its great taste, erythritol is easily digested, promotes healthy teeth, and is safe for diabetics. (Erythritol is also used commercially to add texture to sugar-free foods.)

CHAPTER 2

All Stevias Are NOT Equal

The Many Different Forms of Stevia

Stevia is sold and used in so many different forms that consumers are sometimes bewildered by the choices. This chapter should clear up any confusion about the various forms and uses of stevia, how stevia products are made, and how to choose quality products.

Stevia products generally fall into one of two categories: leaf form or extract. Both have their uses, but it's important to understand what each form can and cannot do.

Leaf Forms

Fresh Leaves

A fresh leaf picked or cut from a stevia plant is the simplest form of the herb. These leaves can be used to make a sweetening extract for sauces and other similar foods; however, the fresh leaves have limited uses. Since the leaves do not dissolve like other sweeteners, they do not work as well in more common sweets like cupcakes or pudding. Please visit our web page at http://www.CookingWithStevia.com for more information on the simple processes of growing your own stevia plants and making extracts.

Fresh stevia leaves work best in herbal teas. Try steeping a few leaves of stevia with mint, chamomile, or any favorite herb or herbal blend, and you will have a wonderfully sweet, flavorful tea without processed sugar or chemical additives. Before you start using the leaves in your favorite tea, however, steep a few stevia leaves in a cup of hot water and drink the plain fresh stevia tea. This will give you an idea of the potency of stevia's sweetness and let you taste stevia's own unique flavor. Yes, stevia has its own taste – most people describe the natural taste as a mild licorice flavor. Refined sugar, in contrast, is so processed that its natural flavor has been lost. Chemical sweeteners, designed to imitate the taste, or lack thereof, of table sugar, still exhibit a faint chemical aftertaste. Natural sweeteners you might have in your kitchen include corn syrup, molasses, pure maple syrup or honey, and like stevia, each provides sweetness and has its own distinct taste. Their one disadvantage is that they all add calories and sugars. Stevia allows you to sweeten food and beverages without adding calories, sugars or artificial chemicals to your diet.

Dried Stevia Leaves

These are simply fresh stevia leaves that are dried to remove all water, allowing for an extended storage period. The easiest way to dry stevia leaves is with a dehydrator, following the manufacturers instructions for drying herbs. Drying them in an oven on the lowest setting will work as well, but check them often, and don't leave them in longer than a few hours. Traditionally, the stevia leaves were harvested on a farm and allowed to dry under the hot South American summer sun. Dried stevia leaves have basically the same uses as fresh leaves.

Ground Stevia Leaves (Green Powdered Stevia)

Like most other herbs, stevia can be ground up. While we add ground oregano for its particular flavor, we only want stevia's sweetness. When stevia was first ground up, the intention was to use the ground leaves like sugar. However, sugar dissolves in liquids, ground stevia leaves do not. Finely ground stevia leaves can be used in the same manner as fresh or dried stevia leaves, but they still fall short when making a pie or cake. I remember making a vanilla pudding with ground leaves, once. The end result was a pasty green pudding that had more licorice taste than vanilla. Yes, you can cook with the ground leaves but other stevia products will help you get the results you want.

Stevia Dark Liquid Extract

(Stevia Syrup)

The simplest form of stevia extract is a syrup made by re-hydrating dried stevia leaves with water, then cooking down the mixture to make a thick liquid. Stevia syrup sounds good, but it requires a little getting used to. A dark, greenish-black liquid, stevia syrup is 100 to 150 times sweeter than simple sugar syrup, depending on its concentration. This is not like maple syrup or corn syrup. The regular stevia leaf has a slight licorice taste; now imagine that mild flavor a 100 times stronger. The intense licorice taste can be very bitter, so use this extremely concentrated extract sparingly. In an 8 oz. glass of water, 3 to 10 drops, depending on the brand and concentration, is enough. This produces a glass of stevia 'tea', but when mixed with coffee, tea or other beverages, it works well. Will these other drinks have that unique stevia flavor? Probably. It depends on the brand of stevia syrup and how much you use. Some flavors, like lemon, can mask or hide the stevia flavor if you prefer.

Since liquids can spoil, some form of preservative is needed. Some manufacturers use alcohol – often 18% alcohol or higher (that's 36 proof-as much as some liqueurs). Some stevia companies use a more palatable preservative such as grapefruit seed extract, chrysanthemum flower, or some other form of approved preservative. Be sure to read the labels carefully to avoid buying products with an additive you might not want. You can even make your own home grown Stevia Dark Syrup.

Stevia Dark Syrup

GROW IT YOURSELF AND THIS IS MOST ECONOMICAL STEVIA EXTRACT EVER!

3 cups of packed, crushed, dried stevia leaves
Approximately 4 cups of water
Everclear alcohol (195 proof)
At least 4 clean 2-oz containers with dropper top, available from the
    pharmacy
Pantyhose, for straining the syrup.
Store bought Stevia Dark Syrup, for comparative testing

In a crock-pot combine 3½ cups of water and 3 cups of crushed stevia leaves that are firmly packed. The stevia/water mixture should be the consistency of mud and may resemble cooked spinach. If the mixture seems too dry add more water. With the lid on, allow to simmer on lowest heat for 48 hours stirring occasionally. Add more water as needed. After 48 hours, allow the mixture to cool. Spoon the stevia pulp into the foot of clean pantyhose. You may want to cut the pantyhose well above the knee if you are making a large batch. Over the crock-pot, squeeze as much stevia liquid out of the stevia pulp as possible (about 3 cups of liquid). With the lid off, gently boil stevia liquid until it is reduced by $^2/_3$. Syrup should be about the consistency of molasses, dark, and supper sweet. This recipe normally yields about $^1/_3$–$^1/_2$ cup of Green Stevia Syrup.

*If desired, you may re-seep the stevia pulp 2 or 3 times. However, this will only slightly increase the end product.

Preserving: Allow the syrup to cool. Using a small funnel, pore $1^1/_2$ tablespoons of syrup in each bottle. Then add $^1/_2$ tablespoon of Everclear. This will result in approximately 25% alcohol content, or 50 proof. Screw lids on tightly and shake. Store away from direct sun or heat.

Testing for Sweetness: In an 8-oz cup of water, stir in $^1/_4$ teaspoon of Green Stevia Syrup. In a different 8-oz cup of water, stir in $^1/_4$ teaspoon of Store Bought Syrup. Compare. You can dilute the strength of your syrup by adding more alcohol, or increase the sweetness by adjusting the cooking time the next time you make syrup.

Makes approximately 4, 2-oz bottles of Green Stevia Syrup

Stevia Steviosides (commonly called White Stevia Powder, or Pure Stevioside Extract)

Steviosides, a group of sweet tasting molecules (glycosides), give the stevia herb its amazing sweetness. With a taste up to 300 times sweeter than sugar, Steviosides have no fat, no calories, no processed sugars and no carbohydrates. Actually, researchers have identified eight sweet glycosides within the leaves of the stevia plant, but the three best tasting are Stevioside (the most abundant glycoside), Rebaudioside A and Rebaudioside B. Since Rebaudiosides A, B and five other sweet molecules occur in such small amounts, they are grouped together under the singular term 'stevioside' for convenience.

Pure Stevioside extract can range in color from creamy off-white with a hint of green to stark paper white. Its taste can vary from bitter, licorice, or saccharine-like to that of super-sweet powdered sugar. The Japanese have been using pure stevioside since the 1970s, and this natural extract constitutes more than 41 percent of Japan's commercial sweetener market. Pure Stevioside extract also provides the base for several stevia products, including liquid stevia extract, spoonable stevia/stevia blends, and quick-dissolving stevia tablets.

Stevioside Quality

The quality of any stevia product depends on the actual amount of steviosides it contains, the percentage of rebaudiosides, the cultivation and extraction methods, and whether or not any questionable additives were present at any time during growing, harvesting or processing.

Amount of steviosides

The quality of the stevioside extract that you purchase is based predominantly on the amount of steviosides it contains. Some 'pure stevioside extracts' contain about 70% steviosides. The other 30% is made up of undesirable plant components. This 30% can give the extract a strong licorice, bitter, or an unpleasant aftertaste. Generally speaking, a stevioside percentage of at least 85% should yield good flavor with minimal bitterness.

Percentage of Rebaudiosides

The other sweet glycosides can also help improve the taste of a stevioside extract. In the world of stevia extracts, Rebaudioside A and B are the gold at the end of the rainbow. These glycosides have incredible sweetness with no bitterness, no licorice taste, and no unpleasant aftertaste. Unfortunately, rebaudiosides make up just a scant 3% of the stevia plant. In Japan, where stevia technology is the most advanced, extracts with a high concentration of rebaudiosides are common. I once received samples of a Japanese stevioside, which was almost entirely rebaudiosides — Wow! It tasted just like 300x sweet powdered sugar. Unfortunately, the Japanese consume as much stevioside extract as they produce, making it impossible to currently purchase this purity in the United States.

As a consumer, you can ask manufacturers what percentage of rebaudiosides their products contain; anything over 20% is good. The highest percentage I've located in the U.S. is 30% rebaudiosides. If the manufacturer doesn't know the percentage, or worse, doesn't know what rebaudiosides are, find another source.

Cultivation

Although stevia grows wild, the most potent hybrids are cultivated on farms throughout the world. Rich in steviosides and rebaudiosides, these plants can vary in stevioside content from 5 to 18%. Several companies also use organic farming techniques for added peace of mind.

Extraction Methods

There exist various methods of processing steviosides and dozens of technical patents describing how to extract steviosides from the plant. The most common methods use alcohol, chemical solvents, gases or water to separate the desirable steviosides from the unwanted plant material. Most often a combination of several methods is used. Water extraction techniques generally create a better tasting product.

After or during the extraction process, some companies decolorize, or bleach, the stevioside. This is an unnecessary step done to give the appearance of white sugar or artificial sweeteners. Natural stevioside should be creamy beige with just a hint of its original green.

Questionable Additives

As a stevia industry consultant, I constantly receive stevioside samples from around the world. Unfortunately, I occasionally receive samples from China and Korea with artificial sweeteners listed as ingredients, or worse, not listed but included in the product, which I discovered only after having the sample analyzed in a lab. Combining steviosides and artificial sweeteners not only hides the bitter taste of low quality stevioside, but also makes the product cheaper to produce, increasing the profit margin.

In addition to artificial sweeteners, other undesirable residues may also be present. For example, in 1999, the FDA confiscated over 8 shipments of "white" Stevia extract powder coming into the USA from Asia because they were found to be impure. In 1995 only four major companies sold powdered stevioside extract. Today dozens of companies are trying to get onto the stevia bandwagon — especially 'mom & pop' outfits that buy low-grade stevioside then repackage and sell it from their homes. They may knowingly or unknowingly be selling adulterated stevioside. To avoid these rip-offs, purchase stevia only from reputable companies with a history of dealing with the herb. If you aren't sure, ask for a certificate of analysis.

Product Descriptions of Stevioside Based Extracts

Clear Liquid Stevia Extract

When stevia users complained about the bitter, licorice taste of the whole leaf syrup extracts, the suppliers started making liquid extracts or liquid solutions with stevioside. Dissolving the pure stevioside into water creates a product that is sweet, concentrated, attractive and pleasant tasting. This is also extremely profitable to manufacture. You can make your own clear liquid extract for a fraction of the cost (see recipe below).

The quality of clear liquid stevia extract depends on two factors:

1) The quality of the stevioside used to make the extract.

2) The type of preservative used, such as alcohol, chrysanthemum flower, or grapefruit seed extract. Check labels to ensure it doesn't contain a preservative you might not want.

Clear Liquid Stevia Extract

BOTH ECONOMICAL AND EASY!

2-ounce dropper bottle (available in most pharmacies)
$^{3}/_{4}$ teaspoon pure stevioside extract
1 $^{1}/_{2}$ tablespoons warm water
$^{1}/_{2}$ tablespoon Everclear alcohol (as a preservative)

Alternative:
Substitute $^{1}/_{2}$ tablespoon Everclear alcohol for water – must keep
  refrigerated

In a small dropper bottle, combine 1 $^{1}/_{2}$ tablespoons warm water with $^{3}/_{4}$ teaspoons of pure stevioside extract. Cap tightly and shake well. Add $^{1}/_{2}$ tablespoon alcohol or $^{1}/_{2}$ tablespoon water

A liquid solution is especially convenient for sweetening beverages and cereals. However, because the sweetness varies so much from manufacture to manufacture, the clear liquid extract is NOT recommended for cooking.

Stevia Blends (commonly called 'Spoonable Stevia')

Simply the best! My children love to eat Spoonable Stevia right from the jar!

Stevia blends combine pure stevioside extract with a filler to make an easy-to-measure great tasting powder. These blends are by far the most versatile and easy-to-use form of stevia available.

Using fillers to tone down sweetness isn't a new idea. When consumers first used Saccharin, they complained that it was far too sweet, so the manufacturers blended saccharin with a non-nutritive filler such as maltodextrin to make their sweetener easier for users to measure. Some stevia companies have followed this example, taking a product 300 times sweeter than sugar and creating one only four times sweeter than sugar (a 4:1 stevia blend to sugar ratio). Although not a formal industry standard, it is the most popular ratio.

Stevia blends are so easy to use. Spoon them over cereal, fruit, or add to beverages. Stevia blends will mainstream stevia as a sweetener for the future because of its wonderful flavor and ease of use.

Types of Fillers used in Stevia Blends or 'Spoonable Stevia'

The following fillers add ease-of-use with minimal caloric impact. Currently, the most common fillers used for stevia blends are maltodextrin and F.O.S.

Dextrose is a common processing agent derived from corn sugar. It keeps other components from clumping.

Lactose is derived from milk; it has a slightly sweet taste and dissolves instantly, even in ice water. People with milk intolerance might want to avoid products with lactose as a filler.

Maltodextrin is a non-sweet complex carbohydrate that is virtually tasteless. Maltodextrin can be derived from corn, rice, tapioca, or other starches.

F.O.S. is the common term for the Fructo-oligosaccharides. F.O.S. are sugars found in a variety of common foods, like bananas, garlic, and wheat. Although mildly sweet tasting, F.O.S. has a very low glycemic index. F.O.S. also promote the growth of some beneficial internal bacteria such as Acidophilus, Bifidus and Faecium. F.O.S. are not toxic. However, some people do not tolerate F.O.S. well. These people may experience gas, bloating, or nausea from the use of F.O.S.

Erythritol – Although relatively new in the USA, erythritol has been the stevia filler of choice in Japan for years. This white granulated powder is derived from natural grains and fruits. It has virtually no calories and a very low glycemic index. Erythritol has the appearance and texture of white table sugar. Best of all, when combined with a high quality stevioside the resulting stevia blend dissolves quickly and tastes almost like sugar. In addition to its great taste, erythritol is easily digested, promotes healthy teeth, and is safe for diabetics. (Erythritol is also used commercially to add texture to sugar-free foods.)

Stevia Packets

Stevia packets normally contain the same ingredients as stevia blends, except in convenient, pre-measured servings. Although convenient when on the go, they are generally more expensive than stevia blends in bulk form.

Stevia Quick Dissolving Tablets

These tablets are rather new on the market. They normally contain stevioside along with other ingredients, and are mainly used to sweeten beverages. Some, however, may only dissolve in hot liquids.

Quick Tips for Purchasing High Quality Stevioside Products:

For best quality, when purchasing a product with pure steviosides, insist on:

1. A high percentage of steviosides, at least 90%

2. A high percentage of rebaudiosides, at least 20%

3. Unbleached, naturally water processed stevioside

4. Organic for added peace of mind

5. Buying from a reputable company

How to read labels

When you purchase a jar of 'pure stevioside extract' the ingredients will usually read something as follows:

(Brand A) INGREDIENTS: 85% stev)osides – stevia rebaudiana bertoni (sweet leaf) *or*

(Brand B) INGREDIENTS: Stevia Rebaudiana Bertoni (96% concentrated steviosides; 30% rebaudiosides *or*

(Brand C) INGREDIENTS: 100% Stevia Rebaudiana Bertoni Extract

By law all stevioside supplements must list stevia by its full scientific name, stevia rebaudiana bertoni. Asides from that, the labels can vary greatly.

Brand A gives its stevioside percentage, then its scientific name followed by a common name of the stevia herb (sweet leaf).

Brand B states the scientific name, then the amount of steviosides and the percentage of rebaudiosides.

Brand C's claim of being 100% stevia is true, but NOT for steviosides. Brands A and B are also 100% stevia.

Brand C did not even list its stevioside concentration. Often, if a brand does not list the percentage of steviosides, then you can bet it is low. Labels can be difficult to read. If you have any questions, call the manufacturer.

CHAPTER 3

Stevia, the FDA and the First Amendment

Why This Book Was Banned!

The Controversy and the Ban

Stevia has been used for 1500 years in South America and is the most popular non-caloric sweetener in Japan. In 1981, aspartame was approved for use as an artificial sweetener . . . around the same time that saccharin was pulled off the market after studies showed potential cancer risks. Stevia's own relationship with the Food and Drug Administration (FDA) remains controversial at best. In the late 1980's, health food stores began selling stevia as a natural sugar substitute. When the FDA received an anonymous complaint about stevia, it banned all imports and sales of the herb in the US. After years of pressure from consumers and the health food industry, Congress passed the Dietary Supplement & Health Education Act in November 1994. This act permitted the purchase and sale of stevia as a dietary supplement – not as a food or food additive. The Act also set forth rigorous guidelines for the labeling, sales and marketing of the herb. Simply suggesting that the stevia be mixed with water could be construed as mislabeling and force a recall of the products. These burdensome regulations eventually led to the FDA's order to ban this book. For more information about the stevia/FDA controversy, read The Stevia Story, A Tale Of Incredible Sweetness And Intrigue by Linda & Bill Bonvie and Donna Gates.

The FDA Destruction Order

On May 19, 1998, the president of Stevita Company (a distributor of Stevia in Arlington, Texas) received a fax from the Dallas District Office of the FDA that ordered the seizure and destruction of cookbooks and other literature. The fax read: ". . . a current inventory must be taken by an investigator of this office, who will also be available to witness destruction of the cookbooks, literature, and other publications . . . Additionally, your stevia products currently in distributor and retail channels with the offending cookbooks, literature, and other publication continue to be in violation of the Federal Food, Drug, and Cosmetic Act. These products are unapproved food additives in violation of Section 409, and adulterated within the meaning of Section 402(a)(2)(c) of the Act."

What was the real reason the FDA singled out these publications for destruction? Mary Nash Stoddard sums it up in her article of June of 1998, published in Nutrition & Healing:

> "Do these books tell people how to commit terrorist acts? No. Do they contain pornography of any kind? No. Do they instruct potential criminals on how to set up a lab to produce LSD or Crack Cocaine: No. The FDA ordered the drastic action because the books contain general information that includes: history, usages and scientific studies regarding stevia – a naturally sweet non-caloric herb with an impeccable history of safe use – and because current federal law requires that stevia herbal products be marketed as dietary supplements without being labeled as sweeteners."

According to the FDA regulations, Stevita Company's sale of stevia-related publications was illegal. Allegedly, the FDA even raided local health food stores looking for the offensive cookbook. It is legal to sell literature about the stevia herb, but you may not place the publications next to the supplements. The FDA took this regulation a step further by saying that Stevita Company's distribution of Cooking With Stevia violated the stringent labeling regulations imposed on stevia. Regulations like these continue to frustrate everyone in the health food industry.

Cooking With Stevia – Marked for Destruction by the FDA

That same day, two agents of the FDA arrived at Stevita Co. to inventory all of the company's stevia supplements, books and promotional literature. Then they met with the company president to discuss the recall and destruction order of Cooking with Stevia. Just as their conversation began, a crew from a local news station arrived. The mood changed quickly as the FDA agents questioned why the reporter was there.

The president's reply: "To record the burning of the books!"

FDA agents: "Oh no, we are not going to burn the books, YOU are!"

President (after a brief pause): "I'm sorry, I can't do that. I don't have a permit from the local fire department. You'll have to do it."

The two agents whispered back and forth before deciding to call their office for further instructions. They were told to mark all of the remaining Cooking with Stevia books by initialing and dating the inside covers of each book. Supposedly, these marks would help keep track of the cookbooks until they were officially destroyed. In reality, once marked, these books were no longer 'new' and could not be sold in the stores. This action was taken by the FDA without a court order authorizing the destruction of private property.

As it ended up, my books were not officially destroyed that day. However, during the following months, the FDA seized all of Stevita's inventory – forcing the company to comply with the recall and destruction order. This action practically put Stevita Company out of business. Only after lengthy litigation was the company was allowed to resume distribution of some publications, but not Cooking With Stevia.

You Can Help

The co-authors of The Stevia Story, A Tale Of Incredible Sweetness And Intrigue, Linda and Bill Bonvie, posted the following on their internet website:

> "Given stevia's record as a completely safe (and beneficial) herbal product, and given that it now may be purchased legally in the country, just what is the FDA afraid of? That Americans will learn about stevia – that it's actually both sweet and non-caloric? Try it? Want to use it? The FDA's prior attempts to control stevia as if it were a dangerous drug had the appearance to many of being a restraint of trade; now that it can be legally sold and used, the agency has gone further and is apparently trying to restrain

ideas, information and criticism of its own behavior – trying, in essence, to act as a sort of 'thought police.' This is a very important issue, which should be carefully followed by everyone – whether you like stevia or not – even if you've never tasted it."

Go to our website: http://www.CookingWithStevia.com and gather more information. Decide how you can get involved to stop the government from railroading this wonderful herb.

CHAPTER 4

Successful Cooking With Stevia

How To Kick The Sugar Habit!

Most of us crave sweets, but let's face it, processed sugar doesn't do us any good. It adds empty calories without any beneficial nutrients, and sugar has been linked to a variety of ailments including candidiasis, hyperactivity, and some types of diabetes. Sugar Blues, by William Dufty, is an excellent book about the problems associated with refined sugar.

Step one to kicking the sugar habit is replacing processed sugar with nature's sweetener: stevia. The term 'stevia' in this chapter refers exclusively to stevioside products, such as pure stevioside, stevia blend, or packets (for the different forms of stevia, see Chapter 2). You can substitute stevia in your favorite recipes by following a few simple tips. Since stevia extracts are so highly concentrated, a little goes a long way – you can replace a whole cup of sugar with just a small amount of stevia. Be sure and follow our conversion charts carefully for the best results.

Tips For Cooking With Stevia

The first thing to remember is that stevia is sweet, but not exactly like sugar. Comparing stevia to sugar is like comparing molasses to honey or maple syrup to corn syrup. All are sweet but each one has a unique taste, and, when properly used, can produce wonderful results in many types of recipes.

The next step to using this herb successfully is understanding how its sweetness differs from refined sugars. Add a few drops of the a non-alcohol stevia extract to a glass of water. Taste it. Its sweetness will differ from the refined sugars and chemicals sweeteners. Add one drop of clear liquid extract at a time and taste after each one until the mixture becomes bittersweet. It is this bitter-sweetness that can sometimes make stevia difficult to work with – you will soon get the hang of using just a small amount.

Some people love the taste of stevia while others take a while to adjust to the mild licorice taste. One way to make the transition is to add little natural sugar like honey, pure maple syrup, or even white grape juice concentrate until your taste buds adjust to the natural sweetness of stevia. In just a short while, you should be able to use stevia alone.

Cooking with stevia can have some limitations. Stevia does not brown or caramelize like sugar. Stevia does not add volume and texture, as do conventional sweeteners. Therefore, baked goods, especially cakes, may not rise as well, and achieving that soft chewy cookie texture will take a little practice. Don't despair – in this book, you will find many secrets and great recipes for successful cooking with stevia.

Helpful Hints

Cookies: Always preheat the oven to the recommended temperature. Crisp, shortbread types of cookies give the best results. For softer, chewy cookies, add some canned pumpkin, uncooked oatmeal or even peanut butter. Never over-bake soft cookies – keep an eye on them in the oven. Another way to achieve a softer cookie texture is with bar or pan cookies like brownies. Their texture and thickness will help satisfy your chewy cookie cravings.

Cakes: Always preheat the oven to the recommended temperature. One secret to moist and light cakes is separating the egg whites and whipping them to supper-stiff peaks before folding in the other ingredients, similar to making an angel food cake. After removing the cooked cake from the oven, immediately invert the pan onto a cooling rack. This prevents the cake from falling.

Flavorings and Extracts: Flavorings and extracts such as maple, lemon, and vanilla are great ways to mask the natural licorice flavor of stevia, while adding depth and interest to your dish.

Dairy: Stevia extracts work great with milk, cream, cream cheese, sour cream and other dairy products. That is why we use dairy products in so many of our recipes.

If you are dairy or lactose-intolerant, try replacing the milk with Almond Milk (see Index), soy milk, or rice milk (both soy milk and rice milk are available at health stores). Vegetable milks work well, but store-bought vegetable milks often have added sugar, so read the labels carefully.

Beverages: This is the easiest place to use stevia. A few drops of clear liquid extract or a pre-measured packet can replace the sugar in traditionally sugar-laden drinks like iced or hot teas, coffee, lemonade, and pre-mixed drink powders.

Breads:

Yeast Bread: A common misconception is that yeast breads won't rise without sugar to act as a catalyst. However, bread can rise with just the flour to feed the yeast; this process just takes longer.

Quick Breads: As with cakes, stevia-sweetened quick breads tend not to rise as well as conventionally sweetened breads. We have made adjustments in the amounts of baking powder or soda in our recipes to give you amazingly delicious sugar-free muffins and breads.

ADDING THE STEVIOSIDE: THE KEY TO GOOD TASTE

(See chapter 2 for essential information about stevioside)

The final secret to successful cooking with this herb is using a quality stevioside product and carefully blending it with all other ingredients. Stevia blends (see Types of Stevia, Chapter 2) are the easiest to work with. If you use a bit too much, it won't ruin the recipe. However, pure stevioside is so concentrated that you must measure carefully; just a pinch too much and your wonderful creation may only be fit to feed to the garbage can. We recommend thoroughly mixing pure stevioside with the dry ingredients before adding the wet ingredients, or completely dissolving the stevioside in one of the liquid ingredients (stevioside dissolves faster in warm liquids). Cooking with clear liquid stevioside is generally not recommended because its sweetness varies so greatly from manufacturer to manufacturer. Whatever the type of stevia extract used, thoroughly combine it with all the other ingredients or your baked goods may not turn out as you expect.

PART TWO

Favorite Stevia Recipes

CHAPTER 5

Beverages

BEVERAGES

Almond Milk – 57

Eggnog – 50

Hot Chocolate – 47

Hot Cocoa – 47

Hot Mocha – 47

Iced Cappuccino – 51

Instant Cocoa Mix – 48

Jungle Smoothie – 59

Kool-Aid® Punch – 52

Lemonade / Limeade – 53

Old Fashioned Root Beer (and other soda pops) – 54

Orange Jubilee – 57

Peachy Yogurt Shake – 66

Pineapple-Peach Smoothie – 57

Sparkling Punch – 56

Spiced Cider – 49

Spiced Hot Cocoa – 47

Stevia Fruit Smoothie – 60

Strawberry Fizz – 58

Hot Chocolate

2 squares (2 ounces) unsweetened
  coarsely chopped chocolate
4 teaspoons stevia blend
  or ¹/₂ tsp. stevioside

or 8 packets of stevia
4 cups milk
Whipped Cream (optional—see
  index)

In a medium saucepan, combine unsweetened chocolate, stevia, and ¹/₂ cup of the milk. Cook, stirring constantly, over medium heat till mixture just comes to boiling. Stir in remaining milk; heat through. Do not boil or it could curdle. Remove from heat. Serve hot in cups or mugs. Top each serving with whipped cream, if desired.

Makes 4 servings.

NUTRITIONAL DATA (PER SERVING): 224 CALORIES; 16G TOTAL FAT; 9G PROTEIN; 15G CARBOHYDRATE • FOOD EXCHANGES: ¹/₂ STARCH; 3 FAT

Variations

Hot Mocha: Prepare as above, and stir 1 tablespoon instant coffee crystals into hot chocolate milk.

Spiced Hot Chocolate: Prepare as above, and stir ¹/₂ teaspoon ground cinnamon and ¹/₄ teaspoon ground nutmeg into chocolate milk.

Hot Cocoa: Prepare as above, substituting ¹/₄ cup unsweetened cocoa powder for the chocolate.

Instant Cocoa Mix

2 cups nonfat dry milk powder
$^1/_2$ cup powdered nondairy
   creamer
$^1/_2$ cup unsweetened cocoa
   powder

5 teaspoons stevia blend
   or $^5/_8$ tsp. stevioside
   or 10 packets of stevia

For cocoa mix, stir together milk powder, nondairy creamer, cocoa powder, and stevia blend. Store in an airtight container.

For each serving put $^1/_3$ cup mix in heat-proof mug. Add $^2/_3$ cup boiling water. Mix well.

NUTRITIONAL DATA (PER SERVING): 188 CALORIES; 10G TOTAL FAT; 9G PROTEIN; 16G CARBOHYDRATE • FOOD EXCHANGES: 2 FAT; $^1/_2$ OTHER CARBOHYDRATES

Variations

Mocha Mix: Prepare as directed, except reduce the cocoa powder to $^1/_3$ cup and add $^1/_4$ cup instant coffee crystals.

Spiced Cider

4 cups apple juice or apple cider
$^1/_2$ teaspoon cinnamon
$^1/_2$ teaspoon allspice
$^1/_4$ teaspoon ground cloves
1 teaspoon stevia blend

or $^1/_8$ tsp. stevioside
or 2 packets of stevia
4 each cinnamon sticks (optional)
4 each orange wedges (optional)

Mix all ingredients together in a large pot. Bring to boiling, stirring occasionally: reduce heat. Cover and simmer at least 10 minutes. Serve cider in mugs with cinnamon sticks or orange wedges, if desired.

Makes 4 servings.

NUTRITIONAL DATA (PER SERVING): 239 CALORIES; 1G TOTAL FAT; 2G PROTEIN; 61G CARBO-HYDRATE • FOOD EXCHANGES: 1 STARCH; 3 FRUIT

Eggnog

6 each eggs
2 cups milk
1 cup whipping cream
1 teaspoon vanilla
3 teaspoons stevia blend
  or ³/₈ tsp. stevioside
  or 6 packets of stevia

Garnish:

Whipped Cream (optional, see index)
cocoa, ground nutmeg or cinnamon

In a large saucepan, mix eggs, milk, cream, and stevia blend. Cook over medium heat, stirring constantly, until mixture coats a metal spoon. Remove from heat. Cool quickly by placing pan in a sink of ice and continuing stirring for a few minutes. Add vanilla. Chill 4 to 24 hours. Top each serving with whipped cream, if desired, and sprinkle with choice of garnish.

Makes 4 servings.

NUTRITIONAL DATA (PER SERVING): 382 CALORIES; 33G TOTAL FAT; 13G PROTEIN; 8G CARBOHYDRATE • FOOD EXCHANGES: 1 LEAN MEAT; 6 FAT

Iced Cappuccino

**WITH A HINT OF ORANGE,
THIS IS TRULY A REFRESHING TREAT.**

7$^1/_2$ cups cold water
1 teaspoon orange zest (optional)
1$^1/_2$ cups drip grind espresso
   coffee
3 cups milk
3 to 4 teaspoons stevia blend
   or $^3/_8$ tsp. stevioside
   or 6 to 8 packets of stevia

Garnish:

Whipped Cream (see index)
cocoa, ground nutmeg or
   cinnamon

Place orange zest in bottom of coffee pot. Brew coffee using cold water and espresso; cool to room temperature. Strain coffee and discard orange zest; stir in stevia blend and milk. Refrigerate until chilled.

Pour cappuccino into glasses; spoon small dollops of whipped topping on each and sprinkle with cocoa, nutmeg or cinnamon.

Makes 10 servings.

NUTRITIONAL DATA (PER SERVING): 48 CALORIES; 3G TOTAL FAT; 2G PROTEIN; 4G CARBOHY-DRATE • FOOD EXCHANGES: $^1/_2$ FAT

Kool-Aid® Punch

1 packet Kool-Aid® brand or other unsweetened punch mix
3 teaspoons stevia blend

or ³/₈ tsp. stevioside
or 6 packets of stevia
2 quarts cold water

Empty packet contents into a large plastic or glass pitcher. Add stevia and mix well. Add cold water and ice to make two quarts and stir until dissolved. If having problem getting the stevioside or stevia blend to dissolve, place punch in refrigerator for ¹/₂ to 1 hour and then stir again. Serve cold.

Note: If you prefer sweeter Kool-Aid®, dissolve more stevia blend into the punch in ¹/₂-teaspoon increments until sweetened to taste.

Makes 8 servings.

NUTRITIONAL DATA (PER SERVING): 0 CALORIES; 0G TOTAL FAT; 0G PROTEIN; 0G CARBOHYDRATE • FOOD EXCHANGES: FREE

Lemonade / Limeade

4 cups water
1 cup lemon juice or lime juice (4
  to 5 medium lemons *or* 7 to 10
  medium limes)

2 teaspoons stevia blend
  or 1/4 tsp. stevita liquid
  or 4 packets of stevia
ice cubes

In a pitcher, combine water, lemon or lime juice, and stevia. Stir till stevia dissolves. Add more stevia in very small increments if you like it a little sweeter. Serve over ice or chill till serving time.

Makes 5 servings.

NUTRITIONAL DATA (PER SERVING): 12 CALORIES; 0G TOTAL FAT; TRACE PROTEIN; 4G CARBOHYDRATE • FOOD EXCHANGES: 1/2 FRUIT

Old Fashioned Root Beer

AND OTHER SODA POPS

1 gallon water
$^1/_2$ tsp. stevioside
   or 4–5 tsp. stevia blend
   or 8–10 packets of stevia
1 tablespoon root beer extract (or other soda extract)
2 tablespoons sugar (to ferment yeast*)
$^1/_4$ teaspoon yeast

In a cup of warm water, dissolve yeast (you can use wine or beer yeast and even bread yeast but champagne yeast gives a better taste). Let stand for 5 minutes or longer to dissolve.

Combine extract with warm water, sugar, and stevioside. Stir well to dissolve sugar and stevioside. Add yeast mixture. You can taste the mixture to make adjustments to sweetness and flavor.

Sterilize bottles in boiling water. Gently pour mixture into each bottle until 1-2 inches from top. Cap each bottle with caps (follow manufacturer's instructions for preparing caps).

Place bottles in a warm area, 75 to 85° F, for 3 to 4 days. Check carbonation. If carbonation is satisfactory, place in refrigerator to stop carbonation process and to chill the drink. If carbonation is not yet satisfactory, allow to sit in a warm area for another day or two, check carbonation, and if okay, chill. When serving, try not to disturb the yeast that will have settled to the bottom of the bottle. Most people do not like that "yeasty" taste in their beverage.

Experimenting: Most soda pop flavorings can be purchased at any home brewing supply store. This will allow you to try different flavors and mix them. One favorite is cherry-cola, which is simply a mixture of the cola extract with the cherry extract.

Caution: depending on the temperature, the carbonation process may be faster or slow; so be careful because the bottles could pop if it is too fast. Since the sugar content is low, the carbonation process is limited due to a lack of food for the yeast.

Makes 24 servings.

NUTRITIONAL DATA (PER SERVING): 4 CALORIES; TRACE TOTAL FAT; TRACE PROTEIN; 1G CARBOHYDRATE • FOOD EXCHANGES: 0

---

*If you are wondering why there is a need for sugar, the answer is simple. Carbonation is achieved when the yeast turns the sugar into alcohol and carbon dioxide. Fortunately, due to the low sugar content and the short carbonation period, the beverage will have virtually no alcohol and lots of bubbles. Also, the yeast will consume the sugar during the process of carbonating the water. Since stevia is not a sugar, the yeast will ignore it and when all of the sugar is consumed, the yeast will die off.

Sparkling Punch

CHILDREN OF ALL AGES LOVE THIS FRUITY DRINK!

1 liter carbonated water (seltzer
  water)
1 teaspoon stevia blend
  or 1/8 tsp. stevioside

or 2 packets of stevia
1/2 package unsweetened
  Kool-Aid® type punch mix

Mix the stevia and punch mix into 1/8 cup of the carbonated water. Stir until dissolved. SLOWLY add this solution to the carbonated water. The carbonated water will foam up so watch it carefully, and go very slowly. Once all the stevia solution has been added to the carbonated water, seal the bottle very tightly, and carefully mix. Refrigerate until cold. Serve cold or over ice. Now you can make any flavor carbonated beverage that you can find as a Kool-Aid® type punch mix.

Makes 4 servings.

NUTRITIONAL DATA (PER SERVING): 0 CALORIES; 0G TOTAL FAT; 0G PROTEIN; 0G CARBOHY-DRATE • FOOD EXCHANGES: FREE

Almond Milk

4 cups water, ice cold

1 cup raw almonds

2 teaspoons stevia blend

or 4 packets of stevia

Soak almonds in 4 cups of water overnight. Combine soaked almonds, water, and stevia in a blender. Puree on high speed for 2 minutes. Refrigerate unused portion. Keeps about 5 days.

Makes 5 cups.

NUTRITIONAL DATA (PER SERVING): 287 CALORIES; 21G TOTAL FAT; 12G PROTEIN; 15G CARBOHYDRATE • FOOD EXCHANGES: $^1/_2$ STARCH; $^1/_2$ LEAN MEAT; 3$^1/_2$ FAT

Orange Jubilee

6 ounces frozen orange juice
   concentrate

2$^1/_4$ cups skim milk

$^1/_2$ teaspoon vanilla

8 each ice cubes

4 teaspoons stevia blend

or $^3/_8$ tsp. stevioside

or 8 packets of stevia

cinnamon and nutmeg, optional

Process orange juice concentrate, milk, vanilla, and stevia in a blender or food processor until smooth; add ice cubes and process until smooth and thick. Serve with sprinkles of nutmeg or cinnamon.

Makes 6 servings.

NUTRITIONAL DATA (PER SERVING): 59 CALORIES; TRACE TOTAL FAT; 3G PROTEIN; 12G CARBOHYDRATE • FOOD EXCHANGES: $^1/_2$ VEGETABLE; $^1/_2$ NON-FAT MILK

Strawberry Fizz

¹/₂ cup fresh strawberries

1 cup plain yogurt

2 teaspoons stevia blend

   or ¹/₄ tsp. stevioside

  or 4 packets of stevia

¹/₄ teaspoon vanilla

¹/₂ cup milk

¹/₂ cup sparkling water

In a blender, blend all ingredients, except the sparkling water, until well blended. Pour into glasses. Add sparkling water and gently stir into yogurt mixture. Serve immediately.

Makes 2 servings.

NUTRITIONAL DATA (PER SERVING): 125 CALORIES; 6G TOTAL FAT; 6G PROTEIN; 11G CARBO-HYDRATE • FOOD EXCHANGES: 1 FAT; 1/2 OTHER CARBOHYDRATES

Peachy Yogurt Shake

1 each fresh peach, peeled and

   pitted

8 ounces plain nonfat yogurt

¹/₄ cup frozen orange juice

   concentrate

¹/₄ cup skim milk

2 teaspoons stevia blend

   or ¹/₄ tsp. stevioside

   or 4 packets of stevia

3 ice cubes

In a blender or food processor, combine yogurt, juice concentrate, milk, and stevia. Next, add peaches a few at a time. Puree till smooth, then add ice cubes one at a time through opening in lid, blending until thick. Pour into glasses and serve immediately.

Makes 3 servings.

NUTRITIONAL DATA (PER SERVING): 101 CALORIES; TRACE TOTAL FAT; 6G PROTEIN; 19G CARBOHYDRATE • FOOD EXCHANGES: 1 FRUIT

Jungle Smoothie

2 1/2 cups pineapple juice,
   unsweetened and chilled
1 cup strawberries
4 whole strawberries, for garnish
1 whole banana
1 whole mango

1 whole papaya
1 teaspoon stevia blend
   or 1/8 tsp. stevioside
   or 2 packets of stevia
1 cup skim milk

Peel, seed, and dice all of the fruit. Combine all ingredients in a blender or food processor. Puree until thick and very smooth. Serve in glasses garnished with a whole strawberry.

Makes 4 servings.

NUTRITIONAL DATA (PER SERVING): 214 CALORIES; 1G TOTAL FAT; 4G PROTEIN; 51G CARBO-HYDRATE • FOOD EXCHANGES: 3 FRUIT;

Pineapple-Peach Smoothie

1/2 cup pineapple, chopped
1 cup plain yogurt
1/2 cup pineapple juice,
   unsweetened

1 cup skim milk
2 each peach halves
1 teaspoon stevia blend
   or 1/8 tsp. stevioside
   or 2 packets of stevia

Combine pineapple, pineapple juice, and peaches in blender or food processor; process until pureed. Add yogurt, milk, and stevia. Process until smooth. Pour into glasses, and serve immediately.

Makes 2 servings.

NUTRITIONAL DATA (PER SERVING): 245 CALORIES; 5G TOTAL FAT; 10G PROTEIN; 44G CARBOHYDRATE • FOOD EXCHANGES: 2 FRUIT; 1/2 FAT; 1/2 OTHER CARBOHYDRATES

Stevia Fruit Smoothie

1 tablespoon oats
4 cups milk
1/2 medium papaya, peeled,
   seeded, and sliced
1 medium apple, peeled and sliced

1 each banana peeled and sliced
1/2 teaspoon vanilla
1 teaspoon stevia blend
   or 1/8 tsp. stevioside
   or 2 packets of stevia

In a blender, blend all of the fruit with a little milk until very smooth. Add remaining ingredients, and again blend until smooth. If desired, add a cup of crushed ice.

Makes 4 servings.

NUTRITIONAL DATA (PER SERVING): 223 CALORIES; 9G TOTAL FAT; 9G PROTEIN; 29G CARBO-HYDRATE • FOOD EXCHANGES: 1 FRUIT; 1 1/2 FAT

CHAPTER 6

Breads & Grains

BREADS & GRAINS

A Better Banana Nut Bread – 67

Banana Waffles – 77

Buckwheat Pancakes – 75

Buttermilk Pancakes – 75

Carrot Muffins – 68

Cheese Corn Bread – 65

Cinnamon Nut Waffles – 77

Cinnamon-Apple Puffed Oven Pancake – 76

French Toast – 73

Golden Corn Bread – 65

Healthy Biscuits – 63

Maple Breakfast Oatmeal – 74

Nutty Pancakes – 75

Oatmeal Wheat Muffins – 69

Pancakes – 75

Pumpkin Bread – 70

Soft and Sweet Dinner Rolls – 64

Southern Biscuits – 66

Tex-Mex Corn Bread – 65

Waffles – 77

Whole-Wheat Applesauce Muffins – 71

Zucchini or Apple Bread – 72

Healthy Biscuits

HIGH IN PROTEIN AND FLAVOR.

3 cups wheat flour
1 cup wheat gluten
1³/₄ ounces margarine
2 each eggs
2¹/₄ teaspoons stevia blend

or ¹/₄ tsp. stevioside
or 4¹/₂ packets of stevia
1 package yeast
¹/₂ cup water, warm
¹/₂ teaspoon vanilla

Dissolve yeast and stevia in warm water. Beat margarine and eggs in a separate bowl. Stir in flour, and then add yeast mixture and vanilla. Let dough sit for 40 minutes. Roll out and cut into biscuits. Bake at 350°F for 30 minutes or until golden brown.

Makes about 24 biscuits.

NUTRITIONAL DATA (PER SERVING): 112 CALORIES; 3G TOTAL FAT; 11G PROTEIN; 12G CARBOHYDRATE • FOOD EXCHANGES: 1 STARCH; 1 LEAN MEAT; ¹/₂ FAT

Soft and Sweet Dinner Rolls

1 cup milk
5 tablespoons butter
2 each eggs
3 teaspoons stevia blend
  or ³⁄₈ tsp. stevioside

or 6 packets of stevia
1 teaspoon salt
4 cups all purpose flour
2¹⁄₂ teaspoons yeast

In a large mixing bowl, combine 2 cups of the flour and all the yeast. In a small saucepan, mix milk, stevia blend, butter, and salt. Stirring constantly, heat till warm and butter is almost melted. Add to flour mixture along with eggs. Beat with an electric mixer on low speed for 30 seconds, scraping bowl constantly. Beat on high speed for 3 minutes. Using a spoon, stir in as much of the remaining flour as you can until dough is only slightly sticky.

Turn dough out onto a lightly floured surface. Knead in enough remaining flour to make moderately stiff dough that is smooth and elastic. Shape dough into a ball. Place dough in a greased bowl; grease the dough completely. Cover and let rise in a warm place till double (about 1 hour).

Punch dough down. Turn out onto a lightly floured surface. Divide dough in half. Cover and let rest for 10 minutes. Shape the dough into desired rolls. Cover and let rise in a warm place till nearly double (about 30 minutes).

Bake in a 375°F oven for 12 to 15 minutes or till golden brown.

Makes 15–20 rolls.

NUTRITIONAL DATA (PER SERVING): 176 CALORIES; 5G TOTAL FAT; 5G PROTEIN; 27G CARBOHYDRATE • FOOD EXCHANGES: 1¹⁄₂ STARCH; 1 FAT

Golden Corn Bread

1 cup all-purpose flour
1 cup cornmeal
2½ teaspoons stevia blend
   or ⁵/₁₆ tsp. stevioside
   or 5 packets of stevia

1 tablespoon baking powder
1 teaspoon salt
2 each eggs
1 cup milk
¼ cup vegetable oil

In a mixing bowl, combine the flour, cornmeal, stevia blend, baking powder, and salt. Add the eggs, milk, and oil. Mix until batter is smooth. Pour into a greased 9 x 9 x 2-inch baking pan. Bake in a 425°F oven for 20 to 25 minutes or till golden brown.

Makes 8 servings.

NUTRITIONAL DATA (PER SERVING): 216 CALORIES; 9G TOTAL FAT; 5G PROTEIN; 27G CARBO-HYDRATE • FOOD EXCHANGES: 1½ STARCH; 1½ FAT

Variations:

Cheese Corn Bread: Prepare as above, and stir in ½ cup shredded cheddar cheese.

Tex-Mex Corn Bread: Prepare as above, and stir in ¾ cup picante sauce (see index).

Southern Biscuits

2 cups flour
1 tablespoon baking powder
1 teaspoon stevia blend
   or $^1/_8$ tsp. stevioside
   or 2 packets of stevia

$^1/_2$ teaspoon cream of tartar
1/4 teaspoon salt
$^1/_2$ cup shortening or butter
$^2/_3$ cup milk

In a bowl, stir together flour, baking powder, stevia, cream of tartar, and salt. Cut in shortening or butter till mixture resembles coarse crumbs. Add milk. Stir till just moist.

Knead dough on a lightly floured surface for 10 to 12 strokes. Roll dough to $^1/_2$-inch thickness. Cut with a biscuit cutter or inverted glass. Transfer biscuits to a greased baking sheet. Bake in a 450°F oven for 10 to 12 minutes or till golden. Serve Warm.

Makes 8–10 biscuits.

NUTRITIONAL DATA (PER SERVING): 229 CALORIES; 12G TOTAL FAT; 4G PROTEIN; 25G CARBOHYDRATE • FOOD EXCHANGES: 1½ STARCH; 2½ FAT

A Better
Banana Nut Bread

1 stick butter

2 each eggs

$^1/_2$ cup buttermilk

2 cups flour

2 teaspoons baking powder

$^3/_4$ teaspoon baking soda

3 medium ripe bananas

$^1/_2$ cup unsweetened applesauce

1 teaspoon vanilla

1 teaspoon cinnamon, optional

2 teaspoons stevia blend

   or $^1/_4$ tsp. stevioside

   or 4 packets of stevia

$^1/_4$ cup chopped nuts

In a large mixing bowl, mix all dry ingredients together. Set aside. In another bowl, mix all liquid ingredients together. Add the liquid mixture to the dry mixture and mix well. Pour into a well-greased loaf or cake pan. Bake at 350°F for 60–80 minutes or until done.

Makes 12 servings.

For a sweeter bread, add one extra teaspoon of stevia blend.

NUTRITIONAL DATA (PER SERVING): 209 CALORIES; 11G TOTAL FAT; 4G PROTEIN; 25G CARBOHYDRATE • FOOD EXCHANGES: 1 STARCH; $^1/_2$ FRUIT; 2 FAT

Carrot Muffins

1 1/2 cups all-purpose flour
1 tablespoon baking powder
1/2 teaspoon baking soda
1/2 teaspoon ground cinnamon
1/2 teaspoon salt
2 each eggs
3 teaspoons stevia blend

or 3/8 tsp. stevioside
or 6 packets of stevia
3/4 cup buttermilk
1/4 cup butter, melted
1 cup grated carrots
1/2 cup raisins, chopped
1/2 cup coarsely chopped walnuts

Mix flour, baking powder, cinnamon, salt, and stevia blend in a large bowl. Set aside. In a small mixing bowl, beat the eggs. Stir in carrots, raisins, and nuts. Gradually fold the flour mixture into the egg mixture till just moistened. Spoon batter into paper muffin cups or greased muffin tins. Bake 375°F for 20–25 minutes, or until muffin top springs back from a touch. Cool on a wire rack.

Makes about 12 muffins.

NUTRITIONAL DATA (PER SERVING): 163 CALORIES; 8G TOTAL FAT; 5G PROTEIN; 20G CARBO-HYDRATE • FOOD EXCHANGES: 1 STARCH; 1/2 LEAN MEAT; 1/2 FRUIT; 1 1/2 FAT

Oatmeal Wheat Muffins

1 cup whole wheat flour
1 $^1/_2$ cups rolled oats
$^1/_2$ teaspoon salt
3 teaspoons baking powder
$^1/_2$ teaspoon nutmeg
2 teaspoons cinnamon
1 $^1/_2$ teaspoons stevioside powder

2 each eggs
$^3/_4$ cup milk
$^1/_4$ cup oil
1 medium apple, cored and chopped
$^3/_4$ cup raisins, chopped

In a medium bowl, combine dry ingredients. Set aside. In a large mixing bowl, mix remaining ingredients. Gradually mix dry ingredients into moist ingredients. Spoon into greased muffin tins. Bake at 375°F for 15 to 20 minutes.

Makes about 12 muffins.

NUTRITIONAL DATA (PER SERVING): 169 CALORIES; 7G TOTAL FAT; 5G PROTEIN; 24G CARBO-HYDRATE • FOOD EXCHANGES: 1 STARCH; 1/2 FRUIT; 1 FAT

Pumpkin Bread

2 cups all-purpose flour
5 teaspoons stevia blend
  or $^5/_8$ tsp. stevioside
  or 10 packets of stevia
1 tablespoon molasses
$^3/_4$ teaspoon baking soda
1 tablespoon baking powder
$^1/_2$ teaspoon ground cinnamon
$^1/_2$ teaspoon salt

$^1/_2$ teaspoon ground nutmeg
$^1/_4$ teaspoon ground ginger
1 cup canned pumpkin
$^1/_2$ cup buttermilk
2 each eggs
$^1/_3$ cup margarine
$^1/_2$ cup chopped walnuts
$^1/_2$ cup raisins

In a large mixing bowl, combine 1 cup of the flour, the stevia blend, baking powder, cinnamon, salt, baking soda, nutmeg, and ginger. Add pumpkin, milk, eggs, shortening, and molasses. Beat with an electric mixer till well blended. Add remaining flour; beat well. Stir in nuts and raisins. Pour into a greased 9 x 5 x 3-inch loaf pan. Bake in a 350°F oven for 65 minutes or till toothpick inserted near the center comes out clean. Cool in pan for 10 minutes on a wire rack. Remove from the pan; cool thoroughly on a wire rack.

Makes 1 loaf.

NUTRITIONAL DATA (PER SERVING): 291 CALORIES; 14G TOTAL FAT; 8G PROTEIN; 36G CARBOHYDRATE • FOOD EXCHANGES: 1$^1/_2$ STARCH; $^1/_2$ LEAN MEAT; $^1/_2$ FRUIT; 2$^1/_2$ FAT

Whole Wheat Applesauce Muffins

2 cups whole wheat flour
2 teaspoons baking powder
$^1/_2$ teaspoon baking soda
1 teaspoon ground cinnamon
$^1/_2$ teaspoon salt
2 each eggs, beaten

3 teaspoons stevia blend
or $^3/_8$ tsp. stevioside
or 6 packets of stevia
1 $^1/_2$ cups unsweetened applesauce
$^1/_4$ cup butter, melted

Mix flour, baking powder, cinnamon, stevia blend, and salt in a large bowl. Set aside. In a medium bowl, combine eggs, applesauce, and melted butter. Beat with an electric mixer on medium for 2 minutes or until well blended. Slowly add egg mixture to flour. Beat until combined. Spoon batter into paper muffin cups or a greased muffin tin. Bake 20–25 minutes at 375°F, or until brown and tops spring back from a touch.

Makes about 12 muffins.

NUTRITIONAL DATA (PER SERVING): 127 CALORIES; 5G TOTAL FAT; 4G PROTEIN; 18G CARBO-HYDRATE • FOOD EXCHANGES: 1 STARCH; 1 FAT

Zucchini or Apple Bread

1 1/2 cups all-purpose flour
1 teaspoon ground cinnamon
1 1/2 teaspoons salt
1 1/2 teaspoons baking soda
1/4 teaspoon baking powder
1/2 teaspoon ground nutmeg
5 teaspoons stevia blend
  or 5/8 tsp. stevioside

  or 10 packets of stevia
1 cup unpeeled zucchini or apple,
  finely shredded
1/4 cup cooking oil
1 each egg
1 teaspoon lemon juice
1/2 cup chopped walnuts

In a mixing bowl, combine flour, stevia blend, cinnamon, baking soda, salt, baking powder, and nutmeg. In another mixing bowl, combine shredded zucchini or apple, cooking oil, egg, and lemon juice; mix well.

Add flour mixture to wet ingredients; stir just till combined. Stir in chopped walnuts. Pour batter into a greased 8 x 4 x 2-inch loaf pan. Bake in a 350°F oven for 55 to 60 minutes or until a toothpick inserted near the center comes out clean. Cool in pan for 10 minutes on a wire rack before turning out and cooling completely on wire rack.

Makes 1 loaf.

NUTRITIONAL DATA (PER SERVING): 164 CALORIES; 10G TOTAL FAT; 4G PROTEIN; 16G CARBOHYDRATE • FOOD EXCHANGES: 1 STARCH; 1/2 LEAN MEAT; 1 1/2 FAT

French Toast

For a custard type center use thick slices of French bread.
If you prefer a crisper French Toast use sliced white bread.

2 each eggs, beaten
$^1/_2$ cup milk
$^1/_2$ teaspoon vanilla
1 teaspoon stevia blend
   or $^1/_{16}$ teaspoon stevioside
   or 2 packets of stevia

$^1/_4$ teaspoon ground cinnamon
5 each 1-inch-thick slices French
   bread
   or 6 slices dry white bread
margarine, butter, or cooking oil

In a shallow bowl, beat together eggs, milk, vanilla, stevia, and cinnamon. Dip bread into egg mixture, coating both sides (if using French bread let it soak on both sides for 30 seconds).

In a skillet heat a small amount of margarine, butter, or cooking oil. Cook bread for 2 to 3 minutes on both sides or till golden brown. Add more oil as needed. Makes 5–6 pieces.

Serve with maple-flavored syrup or other topping if desired. (See *Tempting Toppings, Sweet Sauces, and Great Preserves*.)

NUTRITIONAL DATA (PER SERVING): 110 CALORIES; 3G TOTAL FAT; 5G PROTEIN; 14G CARBO-HYDRATE • FOOD EXCHANGES: 1 STARCH; $^1/_2$ LEAN MEAT; $^1/_2$ FAT

Maple Breakfast Oatmeal

3 cups skim milk
1 1/2 cups quick-cooking oats
1/3 cup dried fruit bits or raisins
1 medium apple, peeled, cored,
  cubed
3 tablespoons unsalted sunflower
  seeds, toasted

1/3 teaspoon maple extract
5 teaspoons stevia blend
  or 5/8 tsp. stevioside
  or 10 packets of stevia
2–3 dashes salt
ground cinnamon (optional)

Combine milk, oats, fruit bits, apple, sunflower seeds, stevia blend, salt, and maple extract in medium saucepan; heat to boiling over medium-high heat, stirring constantly. Reduce heat and simmer until thickened, 2 to 3 minutes. Spoon cereal into bowls; sprinkle with cinnamon.

NUTRITIONAL DATA (PER SERVING): 271 CALORIES; 6G TOTAL FAT; 13G PROTEIN; 44G CARBOHYDRATE • FOOD EXCHANGES: 1 1/2 STARCH; 1 FRUIT; 1 FAT

Pancakes

1 1/2 cups flour
1 teaspoon salt
2 1/4 teaspoons stevia blend
   or 1/4 tsp. stevioside
   or 4 1/2 packets of stevia

2 teaspoons baking powder
2 each eggs, beaten
3 tablespoons melted butter
1 1/4 cups milk

Sift the flour with the salt, stevia, and baking powder into a mixing bowl. Make a well in the center of the flower mixture; add the eggs, melted butter, and milk. Stir until the batter is almost smooth and let stand at least 1 to 2 hours before cooking.

Lightly grease a frying pan with oil or butter. Pour batter onto hot skillet to make round cakes. Cook until bubbles appear on the surface and the underneath is brown. Turn pancake and brown other side. Serve hot.

Makes about 6 large pancakes.

NUTRITIONAL DATA (PER SERVING): 218 CALORIES; 9G TOTAL FAT; 7G PROTEIN; 27G CARBO-HYDRATE • FOOD EXCHANGES: 1 1/2 STARCH; 1/2 LEAN MEAT; 1 1/2 FAT

Variations:

Buttermilk Pancakes: Prepare as above, substituting buttermilk for milk. If needed, add additional buttermilk to thin the batter.

Buckwheat Pancakes: Prepare as above, substituting 1/2 cup whole wheat flour and 1/2 cup buckwheat flour for the all-purpose flour.

Nutty Pancakes: Prepare as above, and fold 1/2 cup finely chopped nuts into the batter.

If desired, serve with Maple Flavored Syrup, Stevia Butter, Banana Sauce, Apricot Rum Sauce, Cherry Sauce, or Chocolate Sauce (see index).

Cinnamon Apple Puffed Oven Pancake

Pancake:

4 each eggs

³/₄ cup skim milk

³/₄ cup all-purpose flour

2¹/₂ teaspoons stevia blend

   or ⁵/₁₆ tsp. stevioside

   or 5 packets of stevia

¹/₄ teaspoon salt

1 tablespoon margarine

Topping:

5 large cooking apples, sliced

2 tablespoons margarine

8 teaspoons stevia blend

   or 1 tsp. stevioside

   or 16 packets of stevia

¹/₄ teaspoon ground cinnamon

¹/₈ teaspoon ground nutmeg

3 dashes ground allspice

1 tablespoon lemon juice

1 cup apple juice

4 teaspoons cornstarch

ground cinnamon

Pancake:

Mix eggs, milk, flour, 2¹/₂ teaspoons stevia blend, and salt in medium bowl (batter should be slightly lumpy). Heat 1 tablespoon margarine in 12-inch oven-proof skillet until bubbly; pour batter into skillet.

Bake pancake in preheated 425°F oven 20 minutes; reduce temperature to 350°F and bake until crisp and golden, 7 to 10 minutes (do not open oven door during baking). Transfer pancake to large serving plate.

Apple Topping:

Sauté apples in 2 tablespoons margarine in large skillet until apples begin to soften, 5 to 7 minutes. Mix in 8 teaspoons stevia blend, spices and lemon juice. Add ³/₄ cup cider and heat to boiling. Mix cornstarch and remaining ¹/₄ cup cider; add to boiling mixture, stirring until thickened (about 1 minute). Spoon apple mixture onto pancake. Sprinkle with cinnamon. Cut into wedges. Serves 6.

NUTRITIONAL DATA (PER SERVING): 128 CALORIES; 5G TOTAL FAT; 6G PROTEIN; 14G CARBO-HYDRATE • FOOD EXCHANGES: 1 STARCH; ¹/₂ LEAN MEAT; ¹/₂ FAT

Waffles

1 3/4 cups all-purpose flour
1 tablespoon baking powder
1/4 teaspoon salt
2 1/2 teaspoons stevia blend
   or 5/16 tsp. stevioside

or 5 packets of stevia
2 each egg yolks
1 3/4 cups milk
1/2 cup cooking oil
2 each egg whites

In a mixing bowl, combine flour, baking powder, stevia, and salt. In another bowl, beat egg yolks. Add milk and oil; blend well. Combine egg yolk mixture with flour mixture all at once. Stir till just combined. Mixture should be slightly lumpy.

In a mixing bowl, beat egg whites till stiff peaks form. Gently fold beaten egg whites into flour and egg yolk mixture. Do not over mix.

Pour 1 cup of batter onto grids of a preheated, lightly greased waffle baker. Close lid quickly; do not open during baking. Bake according to manufacture's directions. When done, use a fork to lift waffle off grid. Repeat with remaining batter.

Makes 3 or 4 waffles.

NUTRITIONAL DATA (PER SERVING): 545 CALORIES; 34G TOTAL FAT; 12G PROTEIN; 48G CARBOHYDRATE • FOOD EXCHANGES: 2 1/2 STARCH; 1/2 LEAN MEAT; 6 1/2 FAT

Variations:

Fast Waffles: Do not separate eggs. Just beat whole eggs slightly then add milk and oil. Add to flour mixture all at once. Beat just till combined but still slightly lumpy.

Cinnamon-Nut Waffles: Prepare as above, adding 1/2 teaspoon ground cinnamon to flour mixture and sprinkling about 2 tablespoons chopped pecans over each waffle before closing lid to bake.

Banana Waffles: Prepare as above, reducing milk to 1 1/2 cups, and adding 1/4 teaspoon ground nutmeg and 2/3 cup mashed ripe banana to egg yolk mixture.

CHAPTER 7

Soups, Salads & Dressings

SOUPS, SALADS & DRESSINGS

Soups

Corn Chowder

1 10-oz. pkg. frozen, whole kernel corn

1 cup potato, cubed & peeled

²/₃ cup onion, chopped

¹/₂ cup water

3 teaspoons instant, chicken bouillon granules

2 cups milk

1 tablespoon butter

2¹/₂ tablespoons flour

1 teaspoon stevia blend

 or ¹/₈ tsp. stevioside

 or 2 packets of stevia

In a large, heavy saucepan, combine frozen corn, potato, onion, water, and bouillon granules. Bring to a boil stirring occasionally; reduce heat. Cover and simmer till corn and potato are just tender, stirring occasionally. Stir in 1¹/₂ cups of the milk, butter, and stevia. In a separate bowl, combine the remaining milk and flour. Stir milk-flour mixture into corn mixture. Cook, stirring constantly, till thickened and bubbly. Remove from heat, and serve hot.

Makes 6 servings.

NUTRITIONAL DATA (PER SERVING): 147 CALORIES; 5G TOTAL FAT; 5G PROTEIN; 22G CARBO-HYDRATE • FOOD EXCHANGES: 1 STARCH; ¹/₂ VEGETABLE; 1 FAT

Cream of Acorn Squash Soup

2 pounds acorn squash
1 1/2 cups chicken broth
1 tablespoon butter
1 tablespoon flour
1/4 teaspoon ground ginger

1 teaspoon stevia blend
  or 1/16 teaspoon stevioside
  or 2 packets of stevia
1 cup milk
salt and pepper to taste

Wash, halve, and remove seeds from squash. Place halves, cut-side-down, in a baking dish. Bake at 350°F for 45 minutes or till tender. Cool slightly. Remove skin and cube. Combine the cooked squash and 3/4 cup of the broth in a blender or food processor. Puree till smooth. Set aside. In a saucepan, melt margarine. Stir in flour, ginger, and stevia. Stir in milk. Stirring constantly, cook until thick and bubbly. Stir in squash puree and remaining broth. Continue stirring, and cook till heated through. Salt and pepper to taste.

Makes 4 servings.

NUTRITIONAL DATA (PER SERVING): 155 CALORIES; 6G TOTAL FAT; 5G PROTEIN; 23G CARBO-HYDRATE • FOOD EXCHANGES: 1 1/2 STARCH; 1 FAT

Tomato Soup With Herbs

3/4 cup onion, sliced

2 tablespoons butter

2 cups tomatoes, chopped & peeled or

1 14 1/2-ounce can whole, peeled tomatoes, cup up

1 1/2 cups vegetable broth

1 8-ounce can tomato sauce

1 tablespoon fresh, snipped basil

2 teaspoons fresh, snipped thyme

1 teaspoon stevia blend
  or 1/8 tsp. stevioside
  or 2 packets of stevia

In a large, heavy saucepan, sauté onion in butter until tender. Add fresh tomatoes or undrained canned tomatoes, broth, tomato sauce, basil, thyme, and stevia. Stirring occasionally bring to boiling; reduce heat. Cover and simmer for 30 minutes stirring occasionally. Cool slightly. Puree soup in batches in a blender or food processor till smooth. Return mixture to saucepan; heat through.

Makes 4 servings.

NUTRITIONAL DATA (PER SERVING): 183 CALORIES; 8G TOTAL FAT; 5G PROTEIN; 26G CARBO-HYDRATE • FOOD EXCHANGES: 1/2 STARCH; 2 1/2 VEGETABLE; 0 FRUIT; 1 1/2 FAT

 # *Salads*

Carrot-Raisin Salad

3 medium carrots, shredded
1 small apple, peeled, seeded, &
   chopped
$^1/_3$ cup raisins
1 teaspoon lemon juice

$^1/_3$ cup mayonnaise
1 $^1/_2$ teaspoons stevia blend
   or $^3/_{16}$ tsp. stevioside
   or 3 packets of stevia

In a bowl, combine lemon juice, stevia, and mayonnaise; mix well. Add shredded carrots, chopped apple, and raisins. Mix well. Chill for at least 2 hours.

Makes 6 servings.

NUTRITIONAL DATA (PER SERVING): 141 CALORIES; 11G TOTAL FAT; 1G PROTEIN; 14G CARBOHYDRATE • FOOD EXCHANGES: $^1/_2$ VEGETABLE; $^1/_2$ FRUIT; 1 FAT

Corn Salad

1 16-oz can corn, drained

$^1/_2$ cup sweet onion, finely chopped

2 each tomatoes, chopped

2 each green bell peppers, chopped

$^1/_4$ cup celery, chopped

1 $^1/_2$ teaspoons stevia blend

or $^3/_{16}$ tsp. stevioside

or 5 packets of stevia

1 tablespoon apple cider vinegar

$^1/_4$ cup mayonnaise

In a small bowl, whisk vinegar, mayonnaise, and stevia till well blended. In a medium bowl, combine corn, onion, tomatoes, bell peppers, and celery. Stir in vinegar mixture. Chill for several hours before serving.

Makes 4 servings.

NUTRITIONAL DATA (PER SERVING): 172 CALORIES; 13G TOTAL FAT; 3G PROTEIN; 17G CARBOHYDRATE • FOOD EXCHANGES: $^1/_2$ STARCH; 1 $^1/_2$ VEGETABLE; 1 FAT

Cucumber Salad

2 large cucumbers, sliced
¹/₃ cup onion, finely chopped
1 teaspoon stevia blend
   or ¹/₈ tsp. stevioside
   or 2 packets of stevia
¹/₄ cup apple cider vinegar

¹/₂ teaspoon dry basil, crushed
¹/₂ teaspoon celery seed
¹/₂ teaspoon dry dill weed
¹/₄ cup celery, finely chopped
¹/₄ cup olive oil
salt and pepper, to taste

In a small bowl, combine stevia, vinegar, basil, celery seed, and dill. Mix well. In a large bowl, combine cucumbers, onion, and celery. Add vinegar mixture and oil. Toss to coat. Chill at least 1 hour before serving.

Makes 6 servings.

NUTRITIONAL DATA (PER SERVING): 99 CALORIES; 9G TOTAL FAT; 1G PROTEIN; 5G CARBOHYDRATE • FOOD EXCHANGES: 1 VEGETABLE; 2 FAT

Summer Coleslaw

1/4 cup red bell pepper, chopped
1/4 cup yellow bell pepper, chopped
1/2 cup carrot, chopped
1/3 cup red onion, chopped
8 ounces cheddar cheese, shredded
2 1/2 cups green cabbage, thinly sliced
2 1/2 cups red cabbage, thinly sliced
1 tablespoon red wine vinegar
6 teaspoons stevia blend
   or 3/4 tsp. stevioside
   or 12 packets of stevia
1/2 cup mayonnaise
1/4 teaspoon celery seed
salt and pepper, to taste

Mix vegetables and cheese in bowl. Mix stevia, vinegar, mayonnaise, and celery seed in a separate bowl. Stir into vegetables. Season with salt and pepper. Refrigerate till chilled.

Makes 8 servings.

NUTRITIONAL DATA (PER SERVING): 236 CALORIES; 21G TOTAL FAT; 8G PROTEIN; 6G CARBO-HYDRATE • FOOD EXCHANGES: 1 LEAN MEAT; 1 VEGETABLE; 0 FRUIT; 2 FAT

German-Style Potato Salad

4 medium potatoes, peeled,
  boiled, and cubed
4 slices bacon
1/2 cup onion, chopped
1 tablespoon vegetable oil
1 tablespoon flour
1 1/2 teaspoons stevia blend
  or 3/16 tsp. stevioside

    or 3 packets of stevia
1 teaspoon salt
1/2 teaspoon celery seed
1/8 teaspoon pepper
1/2 cup water
1/4 cup apple cider vinegar
1 each hard-boiled egg, sliced

Cook potatoes in boiling water till tender; drain well. Cool; peel and slice potatoes. Set aside.

Dressing:

Cook 4 slices bacon till crisp. Drain and crumble; set aside. Cook onions in vegetable oil till tender. Stir in flour, stevia, salt, celery seed, and pepper. Stir in vinegar and water. Stirring constantly, cook until thick and bubbly. Add potatoes and bacon. Still stirring constantly, cook for 5 minutes more. Spoon into a serving bowl, and garnish with hard-boiled egg.

Makes 4 servings.

NUTRITIONAL DATA (PER SERVING): 197 CALORIES; 8G TOTAL FAT; 6G PROTEIN; 26G CARBO-HYDRATE • FOOD EXCHANGES: 1 + STARCH; 1/2 LEAN MEAT; 1/2 VEGETABLE; 1 1/2 FAT

Lemon and Herb Mushroom Salad

$^1/_2$ pound fresh whole mushrooms
3 tablespoons lemon juice
2 tablespoons salad oil
1 tablespoon crushed garlic
1 teaspoon stevia blend
   or $^1/_8$ tsp. stevioside
   or 2 packets of stevia

$^1/_4$ teaspoon salt
$^1/_4$ teaspoon pepper
$^1/_8$ teaspoon oregano
$^1/_8$ teaspoon thyme
$^1/_2$ small red onion, thinly sliced
$^1/_4$ cup celery, finely chopped

In a medium saucepan, blanch mushrooms in boiling water for 1 minute. Drain and rinse with cold water; drain again. In a bowl, combine mushrooms and onions. Set aside.

Marinade:

In a small saucepan, combine lemon juice, salad oil, stevia, garlic, and spices. Cook till boiling stirring occasionally. Reduce heat and simmer, uncovered, 5 minutes stirring occasionally. Pour hot marinade over mushrooms and onions; toss till coated. Cover; chill at least 8 hours, stirring occasionally.

Makes 6 servings.

NUTRITIONAL DATA (PER SERVING): 60 CALORIES; 5G TOTAL FAT; 1G PROTEIN; 4G CARBOHYDRATE • FOOD EXCHANGES: $^1/_2$ VEGETABLE; 0 FRUIT; 1 FAT

Shrimp Salad

1 cup shrimp, cooked
4 ounces cream cheese
2 large tomatoes, finely diced
2 tablespoons mayonnaise
$^1/_2$ teaspoon garlic powder

1 $^1/_2$ teaspoons stevia blend
or $^3/_{16}$ tsp. stevioside
or 3 packets of stevia
$^1/_4$ cup onion, minced

In a large bowl, mix all ingredients but the tomatoes. Gently stir in tomatoes. Refrigerate, and serve chilled. Can be served on a bed of lettuce, as an appetizer on crackers, or mixed with cooked pasta as a salad.

NUTRITIONAL DATA (PER SERVING): 76 CALORIES; 6G TOTAL FAT; 5G PROTEIN; 2G CARBOHY-DRATE • FOOD EXCHANGES: $^1/_2$ LEAN MEAT; 1 FAT

No Chicken Salad

3 cups seitan, cooked (or textured vegetable protein)
1 cup celery, diced
1 8-ounce can water chestnuts, diced
3 each green onions, minced
1 1/4 cups green grapes, cut in half
2 tablespoons fresh tarragon, minced
4 tablespoons fresh parsley, minced

2 teaspoons Dijon mustard
1 each lemon, juice of and zest
1 teaspoon stevia blend
   or 1/8 tsp. stevioside
   or 2 packets of stevia
14 ounces salad dressing or mayonnaise
salt and pepper to taste

In a small bowl, dissolve stevia into the lemon juice. Set aside. In a large bowl, combine all other ingredients. Add lemon-stevia mixture; mix well. Refrigerate at least 2 hours. Use over greens, in a sandwich, or with crackers.

Makes about 6 cups or about 4 servings.

NUTRITIONAL DATA (PER SERVING): 1329 CALORIES; 86G TOTAL FAT; 118G PROTEIN; 59G CARBOHYDRATE • FOOD EXCHANGES: 3 1/2 STARCH; 15 1/2 LEAN MEAT; 1/2 VEGETABLE; 1/2 FRUIT; 7 FAT

Greek Pasta Shrimp Salad

8 ounces rotelle pasta
12 ounces small shrimp, cooked
2 tablespoons red onion, minced
1 each celery stalk, finely chopped
$^1/_3$ cup olives, chopped
$^1/_4$ teaspoon red pepper
10 each cherry tomatoes
$^3/_4$ cup asiago cheese, finely grated

2 teaspoons stevia blend
  or $^1/_4$ tsp. stevioside
  or 4 packets of stevia
$^1/_4$ cup lemon juice
$^1/_4$ cup olive oil
2 cloves garlic, minced
$^1/_4$ teaspoon dried mustard
salt & pepper to taste

Cook pasta according to package instructions. Toss cooked pasta in a large bowl with shrimp, onion, olives, and celery. In a smaller bowl, combine oil, juice, stevia, garlic, pepper, mustard, and salt. Mix well or use a blender. Pour dressing over pasta and mix well. Garnish with tomatoes and asiago cheese.

Makes 4 servings.

NUTRITIONAL DATA (PER SERVING): 528 CALORIES; 23G TOTAL FAT; 30G PROTEIN; 49G CARBOHYDRATE • FOOD EXCHANGES: 3 STARCH; 3 LEAN MEAT; $^1/_2$ VEGETABLE; 0 FRUIT; 4 FAT

Pasta Salad

4 cups ham, cubed
1 pound rotini pasta, cooked
6 ounces olives, pitted
4 medium carrots, cooked, sliced
1 medium green bell pepper,
    sliced
1 medium red bell pepper, sliced
1 medium yellow bell pepper, sliced

1 tablespoon garlic, minced
1 tablespoon Italian seasoning
1 cup Italian Dressing (see index)
2 teaspoons stevia blend
    or ¼ tsp. stevioside
    or 4 packets of stevia
salt and pepper, to taste

Cook pasta according to instructions. Drain. Place cooked pasta in a large bowl. Add cubed ham, sliced vegetables, olives, spices, and Italian dressing; toss till coated and mixed well. Chill at least 4 hours for seasonings to blend.

Makes 6 servings.

NUTRITIONAL DATA (PER SERVING): 517 CALORIES; 14G TOTAL FAT; 27G PROTEIN; 71G CARBOHYDRATE • FOOD EXCHANGES: 4 STARCH; 2½ LEAN MEAT; 1½ VEGETABLE; 0 FRUIT; 1 FAT

Dijon Tofu Wilted Salad

$^1/_2$ pound tofu, frozen then
  defrosted
$^1/_2$ teaspoon salt
$^1/_4$ teaspoon ground black pepper

1 head romaine lettuce, washed
  and torn into small pieces
1 cup Dijon Vinaigrette (see index)
olive oil for browning

Allow tofu to thaw; gently squeeze out excess water. (This process gives tofu a firm, slightly chewy texture.) Cut tofu into 1-inch cubes. In a skillet, lightly sauté tofu in a small amount of oil until light brown. Sprinkle with salt and pepper.

Make a bed of lettuce on a large plate. Spoon sautéed tofu on top of lettuce. Drizzle Dijon dressing over the tofu and serve.

Makes 4 servings.

NUTRITIONAL DATA (PER SERVING): 71 CALORIES; 3G TOTAL FAT; 8G PROTEIN; 6G CARBOHYDRATE • FOOD EXCHANGES: $^1/_2$ LEAN MEAT; 1 VEGETABLE

Orange-Spinach Toss

3 cups fresh spinach, washed & torn
2 each oranges, peeled and
   sectioned
1 cup sliced, fresh mushrooms
2 tablespoons salad oil
1 teaspoon lemon juice
1 tablespoon orange juice

1 teaspoon stevia blend
   or $^{1}/_{8}$ tsp. stevioside
   or 2 packets of stevia
$^{1}/_{4}$ teaspoon poppy seeds
$^{1}/_{8}$ teaspoon garlic powder
$^{1}/_{4}$ cup toasted, slivered almonds

Place spinach in a large salad bowl. Add oranges and mushrooms.
Toss lightly to mix.

Dressing:

In a screw-top jar, combine salad oil, lemon juice, stevia, poppy seeds,
and garlic powder. Cover and shake well. Pour the dressing over the
salad. Toss lightly to coat. Sprinkle with toasted almonds. Makes 4
servings.

NUTRITIONAL DATA (PER SERVING): 312 CALORIES; 23G TOTAL FAT; 7G PROTEIN; 24G
CARBOHYDRATE • FOOD EXCHANGES: $^{1}/_{2}$ STARCH; $^{1}/_{2}$ LEAN MEAT; $^{1}/_{2}$ VEGETABLE; 1 FRUIT;
$4^{1}/_{2}$ FAT

Melon Salad

4 each navel oranges, peeled,
seeded, & sliced
1 each cantaloupe, peeled, seeded,
& sliced
1 each honeydew melon, peeled,
seeded, & sliced

1 cup Cream Cheese Dressing (see
index)
1 tablespoon lemon juice
stevia blend to taste

Combine fruit in a large bowl. Sprinkle with lemon juice. Keep refrigerated until ready to serve. Sprinkle with stevia blend if desired. Top with Cream Cheese Dressing (see index).

NUTRITIONAL DATA (PER SERVING): 226 CALORIES; 1G TOTAL FAT; 4G PROTEIN; 58G CARBO-HYDRATE • FOOD EXCHANGES: 3½ FRUIT

 # *Salad Dressings*

Ginger Vinaigrette

¹/₂ cup vegetable oil
¹/₃ cup white wine vinegar
³/₄ teaspoon stevia blend
   or ³/₃₂ tsp. stevioside
   or 1¹/₂ packets of stevia

1 teaspoon fresh grated ginger
   root
¹/₂ teaspoon paprika
¹/₈ teaspoon pepper

Combine all ingredients in a screw-top jar. Cover and shake well. Keeps for up to 2 weeks. Shake before serving.

Makes about 1 cup.

NUTRITIONAL DATA (PER SERVING): 980 CALORIES; 109G TOTAL FAT; TRACE PROTEIN; 6G CARBOHYDRATE • FOOD EXCHANGES: 22 FAT; 1/2 OTHER CARBOHYDRATES

Dijon Vinaigrette

1/2 cup olive oil
1/2 teaspoon paprika
1 teaspoon stevia blend
   or 1/8 tsp. stevioside
   or 2 packets of stevia

1/4 cup Dijon-style mustard
1/4 cup balsamic vinegar
1 clove garlic, minced
1/4 teaspoon pepper

In a screw-top jar, combine all ingredients. Cover, shake well. Keeps in the refrigerator for up to 1 week. Shake before serving.

Makes 1 cup.

NUTRITIONAL DATA (PER SERVING): 1018 CALORIES; 111G TOTAL FAT; 3G PROTEIN; 10G CARBOHYDRATE • FOOD EXCHANGES: 1/2 LEAN MEAT; 1/2 FRUIT; 22 FAT

Italian Dressing

2 tablespoons parmesan cheese, grated
1/2 teaspoon stevia blend
   or 1/16 tsp. stevioside
   or 1 packet of stevia
1/8 teaspoon salt
1/8 teaspoon pepper
1 tablespoon onion, minced

3 tablespoons parsley, minced
1 tablespoon basil, fresh, minced
1 tablespoon marjoram, minced
1/2 teaspoon celery seeds
1 clove garlic, minced
1/3 cup white wine vinegar
3/4 cup olive oil

In a screw-top jar, combine all ingredients. Cover, shake well. Keeps in the refrigerator up to 1 week. Shake before serving.

Makes 1 cup.

NUTRITIONAL DATA (PER SERVING): 1522 CALORIES; 166G TOTAL FAT; 6G PROTEIN; 12G CARBOHYDRATE • FOOD EXCHANGES: 1/2 STARCH; 1/2 LEAN MEAT; 1/2 VEGETABLE; 0 FRUIT; 32 1/2 FAT; 1/2 OTHER CARBOHYDRATES

Soups, Salads & Dressings

Poppy Seed Dressing

1 tablespoon poppy seeds
$^1/_4$ teaspoon dry mustard
2 tablespoons water
$^1/_4$ teaspoon onion powder
$^3/_4$ teaspoon stevia blend

or $^3/_{32}$ tsp. stevioside
or 1 $^1/_2$ packets of stevia
2 tablespoons apple cider vinegar
$^1/_2$ cup sour cream

In a small saucepan, combine poppy seeds, mustard, water, onion powder, and stevia. Heat just till boiling stirring occasionally. Remove from heat. Allow to cool slightly. Add vinegar and sour cream. Pour into an airtight container; keep refrigerated until needed, up to 5 days.

Makes about $^1/_2$ cup.

NUTRITIONAL DATA (PER SERVING): 300 CALORIES; 28G TOTAL FAT; 5G PROTEIN; 9G CARBO-HYDRATE • FOOD EXCHANGES: 5$^1/_2$ FAT

Creamy Salad Dressing

**THIS RICH AND CREAMY DRESSING IS PERFECT
FOR GREENS OR FRUIT.**

1 1/2 teaspoons stevia blend
   or 3/16 tsp. stevioside
   or 3 packets of stevia
1 tablespoon flour
1/2 teaspoon salt

1/2 teaspoon dry mustard
3/4 cup milk
2 each egg yolks, slightly beaten
1/4 cup white wine vinegar

Combine stevia, flour, salt, and mustard in a saucepan. Add milk and egg yolks. Stirring constantly, cook until thick and bubbly. Continue cooking and stirring 2 more minutes. Add vinegar; stir till smooth. Pour into an airtight container; keep refrigerated until needed, up to 2 weeks.

Makes about 1 cup.

NUTRITIONAL DATA (PER SERVING): 270 CALORIES; 17G TOTAL FAT; 12G PROTEIN; 19G CARBOHYDRATE • FOOD EXCHANGES: 1/2 STARCH; 1/2 LEAN MEAT; 2 1/2 FAT; 1/2 OTHER CARBOHYDRATES

Creamy Garlic Dressing

1/4 cup skim milk
3/4 cup skim milk, hot
1 cup sour cream
1 teaspoon gelatin powder
2 teaspoons stevia blend
  or 1/4 tsp. stevioside

  or 4 packets of stevia
1/2 teaspoon garlic powder
1/4 cup parsley
1/4 teaspoon salt
1/8 teaspoon pepper

In a blender, sprinkle unflavored gelatin over cold milk; let stand 2 minutes. Add hot milk and process at low speed until gelatin is completely dissolved. Add remaining ingredients and process at high speed until blended. Pour into an airtight container; keep refrigerated until needed, up to 5 days. Shake well before using.

Makes 2 cups.

NUTRITIONAL DATA (PER SERVING): 76 CALORIES; 6G TOTAL FAT; 3G PROTEIN; 3G CARBOHYDRATE • FOOD EXCHANGES: 1 FAT

Cinnamon Fruit Dressing

PERFECT FOR DIPPING APPLES.

8 ounces sour cream

$^{1}/_{4}$ cup apricot sugar-free
  preserves (spreadable fruit)

1 $^{1}/_{2}$ teaspoons stevia blend

or $^{3}/_{16}$ tsp. stevioside

or 3 packets of stevia

$^{1}/_{4}$ teaspoon ground cinnamon

In a bowl, combine all ingredients. Mix well. Chill for several hours before serving. Serve with your favorite fruit.

Makes 1 $^{1}/_{4}$ cups.

NUTRITIONAL DATA (PER SERVING): 126 CALORIES; 10G TOTAL FAT; 1G PROTEIN; 9G CARBO-HYDRATE • FOOD EXCHANGES: $^{1}/_{2}$ FRUIT; 2 FAT

Cream Cheese Fruit Dressing

MAKES A GREAT DIP.

4 ounces cream cheese, room
   temperature
$^1/_2$ cup sour cream
2 tablespoons mayonnaise
1 teaspoon cinnamon

1 teaspoon allspice
2 teaspoons stevia blend
   or $^1/_4$ tsp. stevioside
   or 4 packets of stevia
1 teaspoon vanilla

Combine all ingredients in a large mixing bowl. With an electric mixer, beat till smooth and creamy. Chill at least 1 hour before serving. Serve with your favorite fruit. Keeps up to 2 weeks in refrigerator. *Makes about 1 cup.*

NUTRITIONAL DATA (PER SERVING): 216 CALORIES; 22G TOTAL FAT; 3G PROTEIN; 3G CARBO-HYDRATE • FOOD EXCHANGES: $^1/_2$ LEAN MEAT; $3^1/_2$ FAT

Sour Cream Fruit Dressing

MAKES A GREAT DIP.

8 ounces sour cream
$^1/_4$ cup apricot spreadable fruit or
   Sugar-Free Jam (see index)
1 teaspoon stevia blend

or $^1/_8$ tsp. stevioside
or 2 packets of stevia
$^1/_8$ teaspoon ground cinnamon

In a small bowl, blend all ingredients well. Chill for several hours or overnight. Serve with your favorite fruit.

NUTRITIONAL DATA (PER SERVING): 158 CALORIES; 12G TOTAL FAT; 2G PROTEIN; 11G CARBOHYDRATE • FOOD EXCHANGES: $^1/_2$ FRUIT; $2^1/_2$ FAT

CHAPTER 8

Vegetables

VEGETABLES

Gingered Vegetables

1 pound fresh broccoli florets
1 pound fresh mini peeled carrots
4 each yellow crook neck squash,
  cut in ¹/₂-inch diagonal slices

Sauce:
¹/₂ cup butter
1 teaspoon stevia blend
  or ¹/₈ tsp. stevioside

  or 2 packets of stevia
1 teaspoon ground ginger
¹/₂ teaspoon chopped garlic
2 teaspoons frozen orange juice
  concentrate
1 tablespoon soy sauce
salt and pepper to taste

In a large saucepan, boil 3 cups of water. Add the carrots; boil, covered, for 3 minutes. Then add the broccoli; boil, covered, for 3 minutes. Add the squash last; boil, covered, 3 minutes. Drain. Transfer to a serving bowl.

Sauce:

In a small saucepan, melt butter. Stir in all remaining ingredients. Over medium heat, cook for 3 minutes stirring constantly. Pour sauce over vegetables. Toss lightly.

Makes 8 servings.

NUTRITIONAL DATA (PER SERVING): 162 CALORIES; 12G TOTAL FAT; 4G PROTEIN; 13G CARBOHYDRATE • FOOD EXCHANGES: 2¹/₂ VEGETABLE; 0 FRUIT; 2¹/₂ FAT

Sweet-and-Sour Carrots

1 16-oz. bag carrots

4 each green onions, cut into
$\frac{1}{2}$-inch pieces

$\frac{1}{2}$ cup unsweetened pineapple juice

3 teaspoons stevia blend
or $\frac{3}{8}$ tsp. stevioside

or 6 packets of stevia

2 tablespoons butter

1 tablespoon apple cider vinegar

1 $\frac{1}{2}$ teaspoons cornstarch

1 teaspoon soy sauce

Cut carrots into thin slices. Steam about 5–10 minutes until tender but crispy. Meanwhile, in a saucepan, combine onions, juice, stevia, butter, vinegar, cornstarch, and soy sauce. Mix well. Stirring constantly, cook till bubbly. Add carrots. Continue cooking and stirring till heated, but be careful not to overcook.

Makes 4 servings.

NUTRITIONAL DATA (PER SERVING): 122 CALORIES; 6G TOTAL FAT; 2G PROTEIN; 17G CARBO-HYDRATE • FOOD EXCHANGES: 2$\frac{1}{2}$ VEGETABLE; $\frac{1}{2}$ FRUIT; 1 FAT

Maple Glazed Carrots

³/₄ pound small carrots, peeled
1 tablespoon butter
¹/₂ teaspoon maple flavoring

1 teaspoon stevia blend
  or ¹/₈ tsp. stevioside
  or 2 packets of stevia

Cut carrots in half both lengthwise and crosswise. In a saucepan, boil fresh carrots, covered, for 7–10 minutes or till crisp-tender. Drain and remove carrots. In the same pan, melt butter. Add flavoring and stevia. Mix well. Add cooked carrots. Heat through.

Makes 4 servings.

NUTRITIONAL DATA (PER SERVING): 58 CALORIES; 3G TOTAL FAT; 1G PROTEIN; 7G CARBOHY-DRATE • FOOD EXCHANGES: 1¹/₂ VEGETABLE; ¹/₂ FAT

Harvest Time Beets

4 medium beets
2 teaspoons stevia blend
  or ¹/₄ tsp. stevioside
  or 4 packets of stevia

2 tablespoons vinegar
2 teaspoons cornstarch
1 tablespoon butter

Cook fresh, well-scrubbed, whole beets in boiling water for 40 to 50 minutes or till tender. Drain, reserving ¹/₃ cup liquid. Skin and dice beets. In a saucepan, combine reserved liquid, stevia, vinegar, and cornstarch. Stirring constantly, cook until thick and bubbly. Continue cooking and stirring 2 more minutes. Stir in beets and margarine.

Makes 4 servings.

NUTRITIONAL DATA (PER SERVING): 67 CALORIES; 3G TOTAL FAT; G PROTEIN; 9G CARBOHY-DRATE • FOOD EXCHANGES: 1¹/₂ VEGETABLE; 0 FRUIT; ¹/₂ FAT

German Red Cabbage

2 cups red cabbage, shredded
1 small onion, chopped
1 tablespoon stevia blend
   or 1/8 tsp. stevioside
   or 2 packets of stevia
2 tablespoons apple cider vinegar
1/2 cup apple juice

2 tablespoons butter
6 slices bacon, cooked and
   crumbled
2 each red apples, cored and
   coarsely chopped
salt and pepper to taste

In a Dutch oven, melt butter; add stevia, vinegar, and juice; mix well. Add cooked bacon, onion, and shredded cabbage. Cook, covered, over medium-low heat for 20–30 minutes, or till tender.

Makes 4 servings.

NUTRITIONAL DATA (PER SERVING): 184 CALORIES; 11G TOTAL FAT; 4G PROTEIN; 20G CARBOHYDRATE • FOOD EXCHANGES: 1/2 LEAN MEAT; 1 VEGETABLE; 1 FRUIT; 2 FAT

Three-Bean Bake

1 cup chopped onion
6 slices bacon, cut up
1 clove garlic, minced
2 16-oz. cans navy beans, drained
1 16-oz. can red kidney beans, drained
1 16-oz. can garbanzo beans, drained
1 cup catsup (for sugar-free catsup, see index)

9 teaspoons stevia blend
or
  1 1/8 tsp. stevioside
  or 18 packets of stevia
1/4 cup water
1 teaspoon maple flavoring
1 tablespoon prepared yellow mustard
1 tablespoon Worcestershire sauce

Cook chopped onion, bacon, and garlic in a skillet till bacon is done. In a heavy casserole dish, combine cooked onion, bacon, and garlic mixture and all other ingredients. Bake in a 350°F oven about 60 minutes; stirring occasionally.

Makes 8 servings.

NUTRITIONAL DATA (PER SERVING): 847 CALORIES; 8G TOTAL FAT; 51G PROTEIN; 148G CARBOHYDRATE • FOOD EXCHANGES: 9 STARCH; 3 1/2 LEAN MEAT; 1/2 VEGETABLE; 0 FRUIT; 1/2 FAT; 1/2 OTHER CARBOHYDRATES

Cinnamon Glazed Acorn Squash

1 medium acorn squash
3 teaspoons stevia blend
   or ³/₈ tsp. stevioside
   or 6 packets of stevia

1 tablespoon butter
1 teaspoon lemon juice
¹/₄ teaspoon cinnamon

Cut squash into 8 wedges; remove seeds. Arrange in a single layer on baking dish. Bake, covered, in a 350°F oven for 40 minutes. While squash is cooking, in a saucepan, combine stevia, margarine, lemon juice, and cinnamon. Stirring constantly, cook until bubbly. Spoon over baked squash. Bake squash, uncovered, about 10 minutes longer. Baste often.

Makes 4 servings.

NUTRITIONAL DATA (PER SERVING): 69 CALORIES; 3G TOTAL FAT; 1G PROTEIN; 11G CARBOHY-DRATE • FOOD EXCHANGES: 1 STARCH; ¹/₂ FAT

Maple Glazed Sweet Potatoes

3 medium sweet potatoes
3 teaspoons stevia blend
  or $^3/_8$ tsp. stevioside

or 6 packets of stevia
$^1/_2$ teaspoon maple flavor
2 tablespoons butter

Boil fresh sweet potatoes for 25 to 35 minutes or until tender. Drain; cool slightly. Peel and cut into $^1/_2$-inch thick slices. Transfer to serving bowl. In a small saucepan melt butter. Add stevia and maple flavor. Stir till stevia dissolves. Drizzle warm butter mixture over cooked sweet potatoes. Toss lightly.

Makes 4 servings.

NUTRITIONAL DATA (PER SERVING): 153 CALORIES; 6G TOTAL FAT; 2G PROTEIN; 24G CARBO-HYDRATE • FOOD EXCHANGES: 1$^1/_2$ STARCH; 0 FRUIT; 1 FAT

Sweet Potato Casserole

3 large sweet potatoes, peeled,
  cooked and mashed
3 teaspoons stevia blend
  or $^3/_8$ teaspoon stevioside
  or 6 packets of stevia
$^1/_2$ cup melted butter
2 each eggs, slightly beaten
1 teaspoon vanilla
$^1/_3$ cup milk

Topping:

$^1/_2$ cup melted butter
$^1/_2$ cup flour
3 teaspoons stevia blend
  or $^3/_8$ tsp. stevioside
  or 6 packets of stevia
1 cup chopped pecans

In a small bowl, combine 3 tsp. stevia, $^1/_2$ cup melted butter, eggs, vanilla and milk. Mix well. In a large casserole dish, combine sweet potatoes with milk mixture. Mix well.

For topping:

In a small bowl, mix the flour, 3 tsp. stevia, and pecans. Add $^1/_2$ cup melted butter to the flour mixture. Sprinkle topping over sweet potato casserole. Bake at 350°F for 25 minutes.

Makes 6 side-dish servings.

NUTRITIONAL DATA (PER SERVING): 408 CALORIES; 31G TOTAL FAT; 6G PROTEIN; 28G
CARBOHYDRATE • FOOD EXCHANGES: 2 STARCH; 1/2 LEAN MEAT; 6 FAT

CHAPTER 9

Main Dishes

MAIN DISHES

Barbecue-Style Beef

THE GREAT TASTE OF AN OUTDOOR BARBECUE
WITH THE EASE OF OVEN ROASTING

1 2 to 3-pound beef, chuck pot
  roast or brisket

2 tablespoons margarine or butter

2 medium onions, chopped

2 cloves garlic, minced

1 cup Mustard Barbecue Sauce
  (see index)

1 teaspoon chili powder

oil for browning

Rub salt and pepper on meat. In a Dutch oven, brown meat on all sides in oil. Remove meat; replace with onions and garlic, and cook till tender but not brown. Stir in barbecue sauce, chili powder, and 1/2 cup water. Add meat. Bring to boiling, then reduce heat; cover and simmer for 1 to 2 hours or till meat is tender. Remove meat. Cut into slices against the grain of the meat.

Serves 8.

NUTRITIONAL DATA (PER SERVING): 592 CALORIES; 49G TOTAL FAT; 31G PROTEIN; 5G
CARBOHYDRATE • FOOD EXCHANGES: 4 1/2 LEAN MEAT; 1/2 VEGETABLE; 7 FAT

Beef Tenderloins & Greens

1 pound beef tenderloin
1 tablespoon olive oil
$\frac{1}{2}$ teaspoon salt

$\frac{1}{4}$ teaspoon ground black pepper
1 head romaine lettuce
1 cup Dijon Vinaigrette (see index)

Brush beef with olive oil. Rub in salt and pepper; place on a hot grill. Grill both sides till meat is cooked to your preference. Remove from grill and cut into 1" cubes. Wash romaine lettuce and chop into small squares. Arrange lettuce on individual plates. Place beef over lettuce. Spoon Dijon dressing over beef and lettuce.

Serves 4.

NUTRITIONAL DATA (PER SERVING): 379 CALORIES; 30G TOTAL FAT; 23G PROTEIN; 5G CARBOHYDRATE • FOOD EXCHANGES: 2$\frac{1}{2}$ LEAN MEAT; 1 VEGETABLE; 4 FAT;

Pineapple Chicken

1 pound chicken breast, cut in ½" strips
1 tablespoon soy sauce
½ teaspoon cornstarch
2 each bell peppers, cut in fine strips
1 clove garlic, minced
1 8-ounce can pineapple chunks in juice

1 tablespoon tomato paste
2 teaspoons stevia blend
  or ¼ tsp. stevioside
  or 4 packets of stevia
1 tablespoon soy sauce
1 teaspoon Worcestershire sauce
vegetable oil for cooking

Slice chicken into strips. Place in bowl, and add 1 tablespoon soy sauce and cornstarch. Toss and allow to marinate in refrigerator for at least 1 hour.

For sauce: In a bowl, mix tomato paste, stevia, 1 tablespoon soy sauce, pineapple, and Worcestershire sauce. Set aside.

NUTRITIONAL DATA (PER SERVING): 218 CALORIES; 9G TOTAL FAT; 20G PROTEIN; 15G CARBOHYDRATE • FOOD EXCHANGES: 2½ LEAN MEAT; 1 VEGETABLE; ½ FRUIT

Sweet & Sour Chicken

1 pound chicken, cut in 1" cubes
1 tablespoon soy sauce
1 each egg white
³/₄ cup cornstarch
¹/₂ teaspoon ginger
¹/₂ each red bell pepper, cut in thin strips
¹/₂ each green bell pepper, cut in thin strips
1 8-ounce can pineapple chunks, drained, reserve juice
oil for frying

Sweet and Sour Sauce

1 cup water
4 tablespoons stevia blend
  or 1¹/₂ tsp. stevioside
  or 8 packets of stevia
¹/₄ cup white vinegar
¹/₄ cup tomato sauce
2 tablespoons cornstarch
¹/₂ cup pineapple juice
4 cups cooked rice

Chicken:

In a bowl, combine 1 tablespoon soy sauce, egg white, and ³/₄ cup cornstarch. Coat cubed chicken in cornstarch mixture. Heat oil in wok or deep frying pan. Drop in chicken a few pieces at a time. Deep-fry until crispy and golden brown on all sides. Remove chicken with a slotted spoon, and place on absorbent material. Retain about 2 tablespoons of oil in wok or frying pan. Stir-fry red and green peppers for 1 minute.

Sauce:

In a medium saucepan, combine water, stevia, pineapple juice, vinegar, and tomato juice. Bring to boil stirring constantly. Dissolve 2 tablespoons cornstarch in 1 cup cold water. Stir cornstarch-water into hot pineapple mixture. Cook over medium heat stirring constantly till thick. Add peppers and pineapple chunks to sauce. Pour sauce over chicken and serve with rice.

Makes 4 servings.

NUTRITIONAL DATA (PER SERVING): 576 CALORIES; 9G TOTAL FAT; 26G PROTEIN; 95G CARBOHYDRATE • FOOD EXCHANGES: 5 STARCH; 3 LEAN MEAT; ½ VEGETABLE; 1 FRUIT

Variations:

Substitute cubed pork, shrimp, or vegetables for chicken.

In a large skillet, heat 2 tablespoons water over medium-high heat. Add peppers and garlic; sauté for 3–4 minutes. Remove from skillet; set aside. Clean skillet. Heat oil in clean skillet. Add chicken and stir-fry 3–4 minutes or till golden on all sides. Add sauce to pan; bring to a low boil stirring constantly. Add cooked peppers. Serve hot over cooked rice.

Makes 4 servings.

Italian Chicken

4 chicken breasts, boned and
  skinned
1 1/2 tablespoon olive oil
3 cloves garlic, halved
4 bay leaves
1 teaspoon ground ginger
2 teaspoons stevia blend
  or 1/8 teaspoon stevioside
  or 4 packets of stevia

1/2 cup balsamic vinegar
1/3 cup dry white wine
1/2 lemon
1 orange
salt and pepper to taste
1 (24 x 17-inch) sheet parchment
  paper
1 tablespoon pine nuts

Flour chicken breasts and set aside. In a 12-inch non-stick pan, heat olive oil over medium-high heat and sauté chicken breasts with garlic, bay leaves and ginger until chicken is golden. Be careful not to burn the garlic. Remove breasts from pan and set aside. In pan, add stevia, vinegar and wine to pan; reduce mixture by half. Add juices, salt and pepper, and reduce again by two-thirds. Discard bay leaf.

Place parchment paper on a shallow roasting pan. Place chicken breasts on one-half of paper. Sprinkle pine nuts over chicken and spoon sauce over breasts. Fold parchment paper over the top of the chicken. Crimp the edges together until you have an airtight seal. Place in a preheated oven at 375° F for 25 minutes. Remove promptly and serve hot.

NUTRITIONAL DATA (PER SERVING): 596 CALORIES; 33G TOTAL FAT; 62G PROTEIN; 8G CARBOHYDRATE • FOOD EXCHANGES: 9 LEAN MEAT; 1/2 FRUIT; 1 FAT

Curry Chicken

1/3 cup butter or margarine
1 tablespoon curry powder
1 teaspoon salt
2 teaspoons stevia blend
  or 1/4 tsp. stevioside
  or 4 packets of stevia
2 cups milk
1 teaspoon lemon juice

1/2 cup onion, finely chopped
1/3 cup wheat flour
1/4 teaspoon ginger
2 cups chicken broth
4 cups cooked rice
1 pound chicken breasts, boned &
  skinned
chopped chives, for garnish

Sauce:

Melt butter in a saucepan over low heat. Be careful not to burn the butter. Sauté onion until clear; add curry powder and stir until well mixed. Stir in flour, salt, ginger, and stevia. Cook, stirring constantly, over medium-low heat for 3 minutes. Remove from heat; gradually at first, stir in milk and broth. Return to heat and bring to a low boil, stirring constantly until thick. Remove from heat.

Chicken:

Melt 2 teaspoons butter in a skillet. Lightly flour chicken pieces and sauté in skillet until brown on both sides and cooked through.

Make a bed of rice on each plate; place chicken on top of rice. Spoon sauce over chicken. If desired, sprinkle chopped chives over prepared dish.

Serves 4.

NUTRITIONAL DATA (PER SERVING): 1482 CALORIES; 74G TOTAL FAT; 65G PROTEIN; 136G CARBOHYDRATE • FOOD EXCHANGES: 8 STARCH; 6 LEAN MEAT; 1/2 VEGETABLE; 11 FAT

Variations:

Substitute shrimp, beef, or your favorite vegetables for chicken.

Sweet and Spicy Buffalo Chicken

1 pound chicken breast, skinless
   and boneless (or 3 pounds
   assorted wings and legs)
oil for frying

Coating for chicken:
1 cup flour
1 teaspoon salt
1 teaspoon garlic powder
1 teaspoon onion powder
½ teaspoon ground black pepper
1 teaspoon ground cayenne
   pepper

Sauce:
¼ cup ghee* clarified cutter
1 tablespoon Tabasco sauce or
   your favorite hot sauce
⅛ cup vinegar
1 tablespoon powdered milk
¼ cup tomato sauce
¼ tablespoon cornstarch
2 teaspoons stevia blend
  or ¼ tsp. stevioside
  or 4 packets of stevia
¼ teaspoon salt
½ teaspoon garlic powder
½ teaspoon onion powder
¼ teaspoon cilantro

Mix coating ingredients in a bowl. Add sliced chicken to flour mix and coat very well. Place coated chicken on a plate and refrigerate for 45 minutes. Re-coat chicken in flour mix and refrigerate another 45 minutes.

Sauce:

Melt ghee in a saucepan. Add garlic, onion, and cilantro; sauté till onions are tender. Set aside. In another saucepan, combine Tabasco, salt, tomato sauce, powdered milk, stevia, and vinegar and let simmer 5 minutes. Add this mixture to the ghee mixture and bring to a boil stirring constantly until thick. Remove from heat and allow to cool. In a frying pan, heat oil, and fry chicken until golden brown. Remove chicken and place in a round-bottom bowl. Add sauce and toss chicken until well coated. Serve hot.

If you like it spicy, add more Tabasco, ground jalapenos, or try my favorite, ground Habanero peppers; just add your choice to the ghee while its melting.

NUTRITIONAL DATA (PER SERVING): 396 CALORIES; 24G TOTAL FAT; 16G PROTEIN; 29G CARBOHYDRATE • FOOD EXCHANGES: 1½ STARCH; 1½ LEAN MEAT; 4 FAT

Variation:

Buffalo Vegetables: Slice an onion, a zucchini, a yellow squash, a few large jalapenos and any other vegetables that you like. Coat with flour, and fry until crispy and brown. Toss in sauce till well-coated.

---

*Ghee is clarified butter that does not burn like normal butter, available at your local health food store or international market. You may substitute butter but watch for burning.

Crab Cakes

1 1/2 pounds crab meat
6 tablespoons butter
1 each small onion, finely
  chopped
1 1/2 cups dry bread crumbs
3 each eggs, slightly beaten
1/4 cup parsley
1 teaspoon dry mustard
1 teaspoon paprika
1/2 teaspoon salt

1/4 teaspoon ground black pepper
1/4 cup heavy cream
2 teaspoons stevia blend
  or 1/4 tsp. stevioside
  or 4 packets of stevia
1 each apple, peeled, cored, and
  chopped
flour to coat cakes
oil for frying

In a small bowl, dissolve stevia into cream. Set aside. Melt butter in a large saucepan. Sauté onions in butter until clear. Add crab meat, and cook for 5 minutes. In a large bowl, combine crab mix with eggs, parsley, dry mustard, paprika, salt, pepper, and apple. Add cream and stevia mixture to crab mixture. Slowly stir in bread crumbs until moist, firm texture is reached. Shape into small cakes, and coat lightly with flour. Heat a small amount of oil in a frying pan, and fry cake until golden brown. Turn and fry other side till golden.

Makes 12 cakes.

Serve hot with cocktail sauce (see index).

NUTRITIONAL DATA (PER SERVING): 617 CALORIES; 31G TOTAL FAT; 45G PROTEIN; 39G CARBOHYDRATE • FOOD EXCHANGES: 2 STARCH; 5 1/2 LEAN MEAT; 1/2 VEGETABLE; 1/2 FRUIT; 5 1/2 FAT;

Balsamic Medallions

1 pound seitan*
1 ½ tablespoons olive oil
3 cloves garlic
4 each bay leaves
1 teaspoon ground ginger
2 teaspoons stevia blend
   or ¼ tsp. stevioside
   or 4 packets of stevia

¼ cup balsamic vinegar
⅓ cup dry white wine
½ each lemon
1 each orange
1 tablespoon pine nuts
salt and pepper to taste
parchment paper

Prepare seitan or textured vegetable protein according to manufacture's directions. Divide into 4 medium-size patties. Sauté the patties in olive oil with garlic, bay leaves, and ginger over medium-high heat until lightly brown and firm. Be careful not to burn the garlic. Remove patties from the pan and set aside. Reduce heat, and add stevia, vinegar, and wine to pan. Cook until reduced by half. Add the juice from ½ lemon and 1 orange; salt and pepper to taste. Allow sauce to simmer for about 15 minutes stirring occasionally. Discard garlic and bay leaves.

Place parchment paper on a shallow roasting pan. Place patties on one-half of paper. Add pine nuts, and spoon sauce over patties. Fold parchment paper over the top of the patties. Crimp edges together until you have a tight seal. Place in a 400°F oven for 12 minutes. Remove promptly, and serve.

Makes 4 servings.

NUTRITIONAL DATA (PER SERVING): 433 CALORIES; 7G TOTAL FAT; 75G PROTEIN; 30G CARBOHYDRATE • FOOD EXCHANGES: 1 ½ STARCH; 1 ½ FRUIT; 1 FAT

---

*seitan is avalible at health food stores.

Chili

VEGETARIAN

2 (16-ounce) cans kidney beans, drained
1 cup onion, chopped
2 each small red or green peppers, cubed
2 stalks celery, chopped
1 teaspoon cumin
1 tablespoon lime juice
1 cup zucchini, cubed
3 tablespoons olive oil
2 cloves garlic, chopped

1 each carrot, chopped
2 tablespoons chili powder
1 can whole tomatoes
8 ounces shredded cheddar cheese
2 teaspoons stevia blend
  or ¼ tsp. stevioside
  or 4 packets of stevia
8 oz. tomato sauce
2 teaspoons cocoa
1 teaspoon red pepper

Puree 1 can of beans in a food processor. In a Dutch oven, heat oil and sauté onion and garlic. Add green peppers, carrot, and celery. Stir in chili powder and cumin. Cook, stirring occasionally for 10 minutes. Add tomatoes, pureed beans, whole beans, stevia, and zucchini. Allow to simmer for 20 minutes, stirring often. Spoon into bowls, and sprinkle with cheese.

NUTRITIONAL DATA (PER SERVING): 295 CALORIES; 15G TOTAL FAT; 15G PROTEIN; 27G CARBOHYDRATE • FOOD EXCHANGES: 1 STARCH; 1½ LEAN MEAT; 1½ VEGETABLE; 2½ FAT

Seitan Cakes

1 1/2 pounds seitan* or textured
   vegetable protein
6 tablespoons butter
1 small onion, finely chopped
1 1/2 cups bread crumbs
3 each eggs, slightly beaten
1/4 cup parsley, finely chopped
1 teaspoon dry mustard

1 teaspoon paprika
1/2 teaspoon salt and pepper
1/4 cup heavy cream
2 teaspoons stevia blend
   or 1/4 teaspoon stevioside
   or 4 packets of stevia
1 each apple, seeded and chopped
flour to coat cakes

Prepare seitan according to manufacturer's directions. Set aside. In a small bowl, combine cream and stevia. Set aside. Melt butter in a large sauce pan. Sauté onions in butter until clear. Add prepared seitan, and cook for 5 minutes stirring frequently. In a large bowl, combine seitan mixture with stevia-cream mixture, eggs, parsley, dry mustard, paprika, salt, pepper, and chopped apple. Slowly stir in bread crumbs until texture is moist but firm. Shape into small cakes, and coat lightly with flour. Heat a small amount of oil in a frying pan. Fry each side until golden brown. Serve hot with Cocktail Sauce or Tangy Catsup (see index).

Makes 10 medium cakes.

NUTRITIONAL DATA (PER SERVING): 956 CALORIES; 30G TOTAL FAT; 121G PROTEIN; 73G CARBOHYDRATE • FOOD EXCHANGES: 4 1/2 STARCH; 15 1/2 LEAN MEAT; 1/2 VEGETABLE; 1/2 FRUIT; 5 1/2 FAT

---

*Seitan is a high protein food made with wheat gluten and is available at health food stores.

Southwest Peppers

1 pound chicken substitute
1 teaspoon salt
3 each green bell peppers, sliced
3 each red bell peppers, sliced
$^1/_2$ cup Italian Dressing (see index)
$^1/_4$ cup lime juice
1 teaspoon stevia blend

or $^1/_8$ tsp. stevioside
or 2 packets of stevia
1 $^1/_2$ teaspoon cumin
1 each onion, sliced
$^1/_4$ cup water
olive oil for browning

Blend Italian dressing, lime juice, stevia blend, and cumin together for a marinade. Add chicken substitute to the marinade. Marinate in refrigerator for at least 1 hour.

Pour $^1/_4$ cup of water into a skillet. Bring to a boil; add sliced peppers and onions. Salt to taste. Cover, cook for 3 minutes, and then remove lid; continue cooking, stirring constantly, till water cooks off. Vegetables should be tender but crisp. Place peppers and onions on serving plates. Heat olive oil in a skillet over medium heat. Add chicken substitute, and sauté until golden brown. Add marinade and, stirring frequently, allow to cook down. Serve over peppers and onions.

Serves 4.

NUTRITIONAL DATA (PER SERVING): 404 CALORIES; 1G TOTAL FAT; 76G PROTEIN; 39G CARBOHYDRATE • FOOD EXCHANGES: 1$^1/_2$ STARCH; 12$^1/_2$ VEGETABLE;

Spinach and Cheese Quiche

¹/₂ cup melted butter

10 each eggs

¹/₂ cup sifted flour

1 teaspoon baking powder

1 teaspoon salt

1 (10-oz) package frozen chopped
spinach, thawed and squeezed
very dry between towels

1 pint fine curd cottage cheese

¹/₂ pound grated sharp cheddar
cheese

¹/₂ pound grated Monterey Jack
cheese

1 teaspoon stevia blend
or ¹/₈ tsp. stevioside
or 2 packets of stevia

Beat eggs and stevia in large bowl. Mix in flour, baking powder, and salt. Stir in spinach. Add melted butter and cheeses, stirring till well mixed. Pour into greased 13 x 9 x 2-inch pan. Bake for 15 minutes at 400°F. Reduce heat to 340°F, and bake an additional 35 to 40 minutes.

Serves 12.

NUTRITIONAL DATA (PER SERVING): 311 CALORIES; 24G TOTAL FAT; 18G PROTEIN; 7G CARBOHYDRATE • FOOD EXCHANGES: ¹/₂ STARCH; 2¹/₂ LEAN MEAT; 3¹/₂ FAT

Pasta With Tofu

4 cups tofu, cubed
1/3 cup olive oil
1/2 pound mushrooms, sliced
1 small onion, finely chopped
1 tablespoon Italian seasoning
1 pound pasta, cooked as directed

28 ounces tomatoes, diced
2 teaspoons stevia blend
  or 1/4 tsp. stevioside
  or 4 packets of stevia
Parmesan cheese for garnish

Sauté onions and mushrooms in a large skillet with butter until onions are clear. Add tofu and Italian seasoning. Stir in tomatoes and stevia. Simmer for 15 minutes stirring occasionally. Combine sauce with pasta and serve with fresh, grated Parmesan cheese.

Serves 8.

NUTRITIONAL DATA (PER SERVING): 439 CALORIES; 18G FAT; 21G PROTEIN; 52G CARBOHY-DRATE • FOOD EXCHANGES: 3 STARCH; 1 1/2 VEGETABLE; 1 1/2 LEAN MEAT; 2 1/2 FAT

CHAPTER 10

Cakes & Cookies

CAKES AND COOKIES

Lemon Squares

**CREAM CHEESE TOPPING MAKE THESE
IRRESISTIBLE TREATS.**

Filling:
2 each eggs
9 teaspoons stevia blend
  or 1 tsp. stevioside
  or 18 packets of stevia
3 tablespoons lemon juice
1 teaspoon lemon flavoring
4 tablespoons butter, melted,
  cooled
1 tablespoon grated lemon rind

Crust:
5 tablespoons butter
1 tablespoon stevia blend
1 cup flour

Topping:
4 ounces cream cheese, softened
4 ounces sour cream
1 teaspoon vanilla
1 teaspoon stevia blend or
$1/16$ teaspoon stevioside

For Crust:

In a bowl, beat butter and stevia till fluffy. Beat in 1 cup of flour till mixture resembles course crumbs. Press into the bottom of an ungreased 8 x 8 x 2-inch baking pan. Bake in a 350°F oven for 15 minutes or till golden.

Topping:

Wisk all ingredients together in bowl. Set aside.

Filling:

Beat eggs and stevia; mix in lemon juice, lemon extract, butter, and lemon rind. Pour mixture into hot baked crust. Bake at 350°F until lemon filling is set (about 20 minutes). While still hot, spread with cream cheese topping. Allow to cool, cut into squares.

Makes 20.

NUTRITIONAL DATA (PER SERVING): 109 CALORIES; 9G TOTAL FAT; 2G PROTEIN; 6G CARBOHYDRATE • FOOD EXCHANGES: $1/2$ STARCH; $1^1/2$ FAT

Any Fruit Bars

2 cups flour

3 teaspoons stevia blend

   or 3/8 tsp. stevioside

   or 6 packets of stevia

1/4 teaspoon salt

1/2 cup margarine, cut into pieces

1 teaspoon vanilla

1 each egg

1 tablespoon skim milk

1 cup spreadable fruit

Combine flour, stevia, and salt in medium bowl. Cut in margarine until mixture resembles coarse crumbs. Mix in egg, milk, and vanilla. Press mixture into bottom of greased 11 x 7-inch baking dish. Bake in pre-heated 400°F oven until edges of crust are browned, about 15 minutes. Cool on wire rack. Spread spreadable fruit over cooled crust. Bake in preheated 400°F oven about 10 minutes. Cool on wire rack; cut into squares.

Makes about 2 dozen bars.

NUTRITIONAL DATA (PER SERVING): 99 CALORIES; 4G TOTAL FAT; 1G PROTEIN; 14G CARBOHY-DRATE • FOOD EXCHANGES: 1/2 STARCH; 1/2 FRUIT; 1 FAT

Chewy Coconut Bars

2 each eggs
10 teaspoons stevia blend
  or 1 1/4 tsp. stevioside
  or 20 packets of stevia
1/4 teaspoon maple flavoring
1/2 cup butter, melted
1 teaspoon vanilla

1/2 cup flour
1 teaspoon baking powder
1/4 teaspoon salt
1 cup unsweetened shredded
  coconut*
1/2 cup chopped walnuts (optional)
1/2 cup raisins (optional)

In a bowl, combine flour, baking powder, salt, and stevia. Blend well. Beat in eggs, maple flavoring, butter, and vanilla. Add remaining ingredients; mix till well blended. Spread batter evenly in greased 8-inch square baking pan. Bake 350°F for 15–20 minutes or till golden.

Makes 16 bars.

NUTRITIONAL DATA (PER SERVING): 144 CALORIES; 12G TOTAL FAT; 3G PROTEIN; 8G CARBO-HYDRATE • FOOD EXCHANGES: 1/2 LEAN MEAT; 1/2 FRUIT; 2 FAT

---

* Unsweetened coconut is available at health food stores

Chocolate Cake Brownies

FAST AND EASY

3 tablespoons stevia blend
$^1/_2$ cup apricot spreadable fruit or
  sugar-free jam (see index)
$^3/_4$ cup butter, softened
$^1/_2$ cup cocoa powder
2 each eggs
1 teaspoon vanilla

1 $^1/_2$ cups flour
1 teaspoon baking powder
$^1/_4$ teaspoon baking soda
$^1/_2$ cup milk
1 cup chopped nuts (optional)
Chocolate Cream Cheese Frosting
  (see index)

In a bowl, combine cocoa, flour, baking powder, baking soda, and
stevia. Mix in spreadable fruit or sugar-free jam, eggs, vanilla, butter
and milk. Beat till well combined. Fold in nuts. Pour batter into a
greased 15 x 10 x 1-inch baking pan. Bake in a preheated 350°F oven
20–25 minutes or till a toothpick inserted near the center comes out
clean. Cool in pan. Frost with Chocolate Cream Cheese Frosting. Cut
into bars.

Makes 36.

NUTRITIONAL DATA (PER SERVING): 92 CALORIES; 7G TOTAL FAT; 2G PROTEIN; 8G CARBOHY-
DRATE • FOOD EXCHANGES: $^1/_2$ STARCH; 1 FAT

Double Fudge Brownies

6 tablespoons margarine
4 ounces unsweetened baking
   chocolate
$^1/_3$ cup skim milk
$^1/_3$ cup unsweetened applesauce
1 each egg yolk
1 teaspoon vanilla
$^2/_3$ cup flour

4 tablespoons stevia blend
   or 1 $^1/_2$ tsp. stevioside
   or 24 packets of stevia
$^1/_2$ teaspoon baking powder
$^1/_8$ teaspoon salt
4 each egg whites
$^1/_8$ teaspoon cream of tartar
$^1/_3$ cup walnuts, chopped

Melt margarine and chocolate into milk and applesauce in a saucepan. Whisk mixture until chocolate is melted. Remove from heat and whisk in egg yolk, vanilla, and stevia until stevia is dissolved. Taste mixture and adjust sweetness to personal tastes by whisking in more stevia a little bit at a time until it dissolves. Mix in flour, baking powder, and salt until smooth. Allow to cool. Beat egg whites and cream of tartar until stiff peaks form. Fold in chocolate mixture. Fold in walnuts if desired. Pour batter into a greased 8-inch square baking pan. Bake in preheated oven at 350°F until brownies spring back from a light touch or a toothpick inserted near the center comes out clean (18–20 minutes). Cool on wire rack.

Makes 8 brownies.

NUTRITIONAL DATA (PER SERVING): 245 CALORIES; 20G TOTAL FAT; 6G PROTEIN; 15G CARBOHYDRATE • FOOD EXCHANGES: 1 STARCH; $^1/_2$ LEAN MEAT; 4 FAT

Cappuccino Fudge Brownies

6 tablespoons butter

1 tablespoons instant coffee crystals

3 tablespoons cocoa

3 tablespoons stevia blend

or 1 tsp. stevioside

or 18 packets of stevia

1/3 cup skim milk

1/3 cup unsweetened applesauce

1 each egg yolk

1 teaspoon vanilla

2/3 cup flour

1/2 teaspoon baking powder

1/8 teaspoon salt

4 each egg whites

1/8 teaspoon cream of tartar

1/3 cup walnuts, chopped

In a heavy saucepan, combine margarine, stevia, instant coffee crystals, cocoa, milk, and applesauce. Heat until margarine melts, then whisk mixture until stevia dissolves. Remove from heat and whisk in egg yolk and vanilla. Taste mixture and adjust sweetness to personal tastes, if necessary, by whisking in more stevia a tiny bit at a time till it dissolves. Mix in flour, baking powder, and salt until smooth. Allow to cool.

In a large mixing bowl, beat egg whites and cream of tartar until stiff peaks are formed. Fold in chocolate mixture and walnuts. Pour batter into a greased 8-inch square baking pan. Bake in preheated oven at 350°F until brownies bounce back after light touch or a toothpick inserted near the center comes out clean (18–20 minutes). Cut into squares.

Makes 16 brownies.

NUTRITIONAL DATA (PER SERVING): 90 CALORIES; 6G TOTAL FAT; 3G PROTEIN; 6G CARBOHYDRATE • FOOD EXCHANGES: 1/2 STARCH; 1 FAT

Buttery Shortbread Cookies

1 ¼ cups flour   *or* 5 packets of stevia
2 ½ teaspoons stevia blend   ¼ teaspoon salt
   or ⁵/₁₆ tsp. stevioside   ½ cup butter

In a mixing bowl, combine flour, salt, and stevia. Cut in butter till
mixture resembles fine crumbs and starts to cling. Form the mixture
into a ball; knead till smooth. On an ungreased cookie sheet, pat or
roll the dough into an 8-inch circle. Using your fingers, press to make
a scalloped edge. With a knife, cut circle into 16 pie-shaped wedges,
leaving wedges in the circle shape. Bake in a 325°F oven for 25–30
minutes or till bottom just starts to brown and center is set. While
warm, cut circle into wedges again. Cool on the cookie sheet for 5
minutes. Remove from cookie sheet; cool on a wire rack.

Makes 16 wedges.

NUTRITIONAL DATA (PER SERVING): 86 CALORIES; 6G TOTAL FAT; 1G PROTEIN; 7G CARBOHY-
DRATE • FOOD EXCHANGES: ½ STARCH; 1 FAT

Pecan Sandies

THESE SCRUMPTIOUS COOKIES
WILL BE A HIT AT ANY PARTY.

1 cup butter
2¼ cups all purpose flour
4 teaspoons stevia blend
   or ½ tsp. stevioside
   or 8 packets of stevia
1 teaspoon vanilla
1 cup pecans, finely chopped

Coating:
1 cup finely chopped pecans
1 teaspoon stevia blend
   or ⅛ tsp. stevioside
   or 2 packets of stevia

In a mixing bowl, beat butter with an electric mixer on medium to high speed for 30 seconds. Add about half of the flour, 4 teaspoons stevia blend, vanilla, and 1 tablespoon water. Beat till thoroughly combined. Beat in remaining flour. Stir in 1 cup of finely chopped pecans. In a separate bowl, combine 1 cup finely chopped pecans with 1 teaspoon stevia. Shape dough into crescents, 1-inch balls or 2-inch fingers. Press into pecan mixture covering the cookies completely. Place on an ungreased cookie sheet. Bake in a 325°F oven about 20 minutes or till bottoms are lightly browned. Cool cookies on a wire rack.

Makes about 3 dozen cookies.

NUTRITIONAL DATA (PER SERVING): 96 CALORIES; 7G TOTAL FAT; 1G PROTEIN; 7G CARBOHYDRATE • FOOD EXCHANGES: ½ STARCH; 1½ FAT

Cream Cheese Cookies

YOU CAN MAKE FUN SHAPE WITH THESE COOKIES.

$^1/_2$ cup butter

8 ounces cream cheese, softened

2 cups flour

1 each egg

$^1/_2$ teaspoon baking powder

$^1/_2$ teaspoon vanilla

3$^1/_2$ tablespoons stevia blend

or $^3/_4$ tsp. stevioside

or 7 packets of stevia

Beat stevia, vanilla, butter, cream cheese, and egg in a bowl till fluffy. Add dry ingredients. Choose one of the following methods to shape cookies:

Method 1: Shape dough into 1-inch balls. Place 2 inches apart on greased cookie sheet. Using the bottom of a drinking glass press balls flat.

Method 2: Chill dough, roll out, and cut into desired shapes.

Bake in a preheated oven at 375°F for 8–10 minutes. Cool on a wire rack.

Makes about 60 cookies.

NUTRITIONAL DATA (PER SERVING): 43 CALORIES; 3G TOTAL FAT; 1G PROTEIN; 3G CARBOHY-DRATE • FOOD EXCHANGES: $^1/_2$ FAT

Variation:

Chocolate Cream Cheese Cookies: Prepare as above, except in a double boiler combine 2 ounces unsweetened bakers chocolate and 1 tablespoon stevia blend. Stir over medium heat till smooth. Add chocolate mixture to cream cheese.

Fruity Cookies

A LOVELY SURPRISE INSIDE EACH COOKIE.

1 cup margarine, softened

1 8-oz. package cream cheese, softened

3 teaspoons stevia blend
   or ³/₈ tsp. stevioside

or 6 packets of stevia

2 cups flour

¹/₄ teaspoon salt

¹/₄ cup spreadable fruit or sugar-free jam

Beat margarine, cream cheese, and stevia until fluffy; mix in flour and salt to form a soft dough. Cover, and refrigerate until dough is firm. Roll dough on lightly floured surface into circles ¹/₈ inch thick; cut into 3-inch circles. Place ¹/₄ teaspoon of spreadable fruit in center of each round; fold rounds into halves. Seal edges with a fork. Pierce tops of cookies with knife. Bake cookies on greased cookie sheets in 350°F oven until lightly browned (about 8–10 minutes). Cool on wire racks.

Makes about 3 dozen.

NUTRITIONAL DATA (PER SERVING): 96 CALORIES; 7G TOTAL FAT; 1G PROTEIN; 7G CARBOHYDRATE • FOOD EXCHANGES: ¹/₂ STARCH; 1 ¹/₂ FAT

Meringue Cookie Treats

**CONTAINS 0 FAT AND LOW CARBOHYDRATES –
THAT'S A TREAT!**

2 tablespoons nonfat powdered
  milk
3 teaspoons stevia blend
  or 3/8 tsp. stevioside
  or 6 packets of stevia

2 each egg whites, at room
  temperature
1/4 teaspoon cream of tartar
1/4 teaspoon vanilla, to taste

Mix dry ingredients together. In a separate bowl, beat egg whites. While beating, slowly add the dry ingredients. Beat until mixture is super-stiff. This can take up to 10 minutes. You can not over-beat egg whites. Add vanilla and mix just until blended. Place small, half-teaspoon-size drops on oiled parchment paper. You can use a pastry bag to make the drops. Bake in preheated oven at 350°F until dry all the way through and slightly golden (about 25 minutes). Remove from oven, and allow to cool. Store in an airtight container.

Makes about 45 cookies.

NUTRITIONAL DATA (PER SERVING): 3 CALORIES; TRACE TOTAL FAT; TRACE PROTEIN; TRACE CARBOHYDRATE • FOOD EXCHANGES: FREE

Peanut Butter Cookies

$^{1}/_{2}$ cup butter

$^{3}/_{4}$ cup creamy natural peanut
   butter

2 tablespoons stevia blend
   or $^{3}/_{4}$ tsp. stevioside
   or 12 packets of stevia

$^{1}/_{4}$ cup milk

1 each egg

1 teaspoon vanilla extract

1$^{1}/_{2}$ cups flour

1 teaspoon baking soda

$^{1}/_{2}$ teaspoon baking powder

$^{1}/_{2}$ teaspoon vanilla

$^{3}/_{4}$ cup chopped roasted peanuts
   (optional)

In a small bowl, combine stevia, flour, baking soda, and baking powder; mix well. In another bowl, combine butter and peanut butter; beat till fluffy. Beat egg, milk, and vanilla into peanut butter mixture. Slowly add dry ingredients to wet ingredients. Beat till thoroughly combined. Shape dough into 1-inch balls. Place 2 inches apart on an ungreased cookie sheet. Flatten by crisscrossing with the tines of a fork. Bake in a 375°F oven for 7 to 9 minutes or till bottoms are lightly browned. Cool cookies on a wire rack.

Makes about 36.

◄NUTRITIONAL DATA (PER SERVING): 94 CALORIES; 7G TOTAL FAT; 3G PROTEIN; 6G CARBOHYDRATE • FOOD EXCHANGES: $^{1}/_{2}$ STARCH; 1 FAT

Pumpkin Spice Cookies

MOIST AND CHEWY PERFECTLY SPICED COOKIES.

1/2 cup margarine, softened
7 teaspoons stevia blend
  or 7/8 tsp. stevioside
  or 14 packets of stevia
1 cup canned pumpkin
2 cups all purpose flour
1 teaspoon baking soda

1/4 teaspoon salt
1 1/2 teaspoons ground cinnamon
1/2 teaspoon ground cloves
1/2 teaspoon ground nutmeg
1/8 teaspoon ground ginger
1/2 cup sour cream
1/2 cup raisins, finely chopped

Beat margarine and stevia until fluffy in large bowl; beat in pumpkin. Mix in flour, baking soda, salt, and spices alternately with sour cream. Mix in raisins. Spoon batter by heaping teaspoons onto greased cookie sheets. Bake cookies in preheated 375°F oven until browned (10 to 12 minutes).

Makes 24 cookies.

NUTRITIONAL DATA (PER SERVING): 95 CALORIES; 5G TOTAL FAT; 1G PROTEIN; 12G CARBOHY-DRATE • FOOD EXCHANGES: 1/2 STARCH; 1 FAT

Angel Food Cake

11 large egg whites, at room
temperature
3 tablespoons stevia blend
or 1 tsp. stevioside
or 18 packets of stevia
1 cup cake flour

2 tablespoons stevia blend
or 3/4 tsp. stevioside
or 12 packets of stevia
1 1/2 teaspoons cream of tartar
1 teaspoon vanilla

Sift 2 tablespoons stevia blend and flour together. Set aside. In a large
bowl, beat egg whites, cream of tartar, and 3 tablespoons stevia blend
till stiff peaks form. Slowly sift about one-third flour mixture over stiff
egg whites; fold in. Continue sifting and folding remaining flour mixture. Pour into an ungreased, 10-inch tube pan. Bake at 350°F for 40
to 45 minutes or till top springs back from a light touch. Immediately
invert cake – leave in pan. This helps prevent the cake from falling.
Allow to cool completely. Loosen sides of cake from pan with a knife;
remove cake.

Makes 12 servings.

NUTRITIONAL DATA (PER SERVING): 50 CALORIES; TRACE TOTAL FAT; 4G PROTEIN; 8G
CARBOHYDRATE • FOOD EXCHANGES: 1/2 STARCH; 1/2 LEAN MEAT

Hot-Milk Cake

1 cup cake flour
1 teaspoon baking powder
$^{1}/_{2}$ teaspoon baking soda
2 each eggs
5 teaspoons stevia blend

or $^{5}/_{8}$ tsp. stevioside
or 10 packets of stevia
$^{1}/_{2}$ cup milk
2 teaspoons margarine

In a small bowl, combine flour and baking powder. In another bowl, beat eggs with an electric mixer on high speed about 4 minutes. Gradually add stevia; beat at medium speed for 4 to 5 minutes or till light and fluffy. Add flour mixture; beat at low-to-medium speed just till combined.

In a saucepan, stirring constantly, heat margarine till it melts; add to batter, beating till combined. Pour into a greased 9 x 9 x 2-inch baking pan. Bake in a 350°F oven for 20 to 25 minutes or till a toothpick comes out clean.

Makes 9 servings.

NUTRITIONAL DATA (PER SERVING): 75 CALORIES; 2G TOTAL FAT; 3G PROTEIN; 10G CARBOHY-DRATE • FOOD EXCHANGES: $^{1}/_{2}$ STARCH; $^{1}/_{2}$ FAT

Lemon Cake

¼ cup margarine
2½ teaspoons stevia blend
   or ⁵⁄₁₆ tsp. stevioside
   or 5 packets of stevia
1 each egg

1 cup cake flour
½ teaspoon baking soda
1½ teaspoons baking powder
½ cup nonfat sour cream
5 teaspoons lemon juice

Cream butter with stevia blend and egg until fluffy. In a separate bowl, stir together flour, baking powder, and baking soda. In another bowl, combine sour cream with lemon juice. Add dry ingredients to creamed mixture alternately with liquid ingredients. Pour batter into a greased and floured, 9-inch cake pan. Bake in a preheated 350°F oven until golden and a toothpick inserted in the center comes out clean (about 25 minutes).

Makes 6 servings.

NUTRITIONAL DATA (PER SERVING): 159 CALORIES; 8G TOTAL FAT; 4G PROTEIN; 17G CARBO-HYDRATE • FOOD EXCHANGES: 1 STARCH; ½ LEAN MEAT; 1½ FAT; ½ OTHER CARBOHY-DRATES

Lemon-Orange Sponge Cake

6 each egg yolks
$^{1}/_{2}$ cup sour cream
1 teaspoon orange extract
1 teaspoon lemon juice
1 teaspoon vanilla
5 teaspoons stevia blend
   or $^{5}/_{8}$ tsp. stevioside

   or 10 packets of stevia
1 $^{1}/_{4}$ cups cake flour
6 each egg whites
$^{1}/_{2}$ teaspoon cream of tartar
2 teaspoons stevia blend
   or $^{1}/_{4}$ tsp. stevioside
   or 4 packets of stevia

In a bowl, beat stevia blend, egg yolks, sour cream, orange extract, lemon extract, and vanilla with an electric mixer on high until well mixed and fluffy. Slowly beat in the flour. Set the yolk mixture aside. Wash beaters. In a large bowl, beat egg whites, and cream of tartar at medium speed until soft peaks form. Sprinkle 2 teaspoons of stevia blend over the egg whites. Beat at high speed until stiff peaks form. Fold 1 cup of the beaten egg white mixture into the yolk mixture; fold yolk mixture into remaining white mixture. Pour into an ungreased, 10-inch tube pan. Bake in a 325°F oven for 55–65 minutes or till golden brown. Leaving cake in pan, quickly invert cake. This is to prevent the cake from falling. Cool thoroughly. Use a knife to loosen sides of cake from pan; remove cake from pan.

Makes 12 servings.

NUTRITIONAL DATA (PER SERVING): 102 CALORIES; 5G TOTAL FAT; 4G PROTEIN; 10G CARBO-HYDRATE • FOOD EXCHANGES: $^{1}/_{2}$ STARCH; $^{1}/_{2}$ LEAN MEAT; 1 FAT

Pineapple Upside-Down Cake

1 14-oz. can unsweetened crushed pineapple in juice, undrained
2½ teaspoons lemon juice
2 teaspoons stevia blend
  or ¼ tsp. stevioside
  or 4 packets of stevia
1½ teaspoons cornstarch
4 teaspoons margarine, at room temperature
2 teaspoons stevia blend
  or ¼ tsp. stevioside
  or 4 packets of stevia
1 each egg
1 cup cake flour
1 teaspoon baking soda
1 teaspoon baking powder
¼ teaspoon cinnamon
¼ teaspoon nutmeg
¼ teaspoon ginger
1 teaspoon vanilla
¼ cup buttermilk

Drain pineapple, saving ½ cup juice. Mix pineapple, 1 teaspoon lemon juice, stevia blend, and cornstarch. Spread mixture evenly in the bottom of an 8-inch, square cake pan. Next, beat margarine and stevia blend in medium bowl until fluffy; beat in egg. In small bowl, combine flour, baking powder, baking soda, and spices. Combine ½ cup pineapple juice and remaining 1 teaspoon lemon juice; add to margarine mixture alternating with buttermilk. Spread batter over pineapple mixture in cake pan. Bake in preheated 350°F oven until browned and toothpick inserted in center comes out clean (about 25 minutes). Invert cake immediately onto serving plate.

Makes 8 servings.

NUTRITIONAL DATA (PER SERVING): 113 CALORIES; 3G TOTAL FAT; 2G PROTEIN; 20G CARBOHYDRATE • FOOD EXCHANGES: 1 STARCH; ½ FRUIT; ½ FAT

Strawberry Shortcake

6 cups sliced strawberries
2 tablespoons stevia blend
  or $^3/_4$ tsp. stevioside
  or 12 packets of stevia
2 cups flour
2 teaspoons baking powder
2 tablespoons stevia blend

or $^3/_4$ tsp. stevioside
or 12 packets of stevia
$^1/_2$ cup butter
1 each egg, beaten
$^2/_3$ cup milk
Whipped Cream (see index)

In a medium bowl, stir together strawberries and 2 tablespoons stevia blend. Set aside. In another bowl, stir together 2 tablespoons stevia blend, flour, and baking powder. Cut in margarine; add egg and milk. Stir just until moist. Spread into a greased 8 x 1$^1/_2$-inch round, baking pan. Bake at 450°F for 15 to 20 minutes or till toothpick inserted in center comes out clean. Cool in pan. Remove from pan. Divide into 2 layers. Spoon the strawberry mixture between layers and over top. Top with Whipped Cream. Serve immediately.

Makes 8 servings.

NUTRITIONAL DATA (PER SERVING): 270 CALORIES; 13G TOTAL FAT; 5G PROTEIN; 33G CARBOHYDRATE • FOOD EXCHANGES: 1$^1/_2$ STARCH; $^1/_2$ FRUIT; 2$^1/_2$ FAT

Cinnamon Swirl Coffee Cake

4 tablespoons margarine, softened
8 teaspoons stevia blend
   or 1 tsp. stevioside
   or 16 packets of stevia
1 each egg
$^1/_4$ cup sour cream

2 teaspoons maple flavoring
$2^3/_4$ cups cake flour
4 teaspoons baking powder
$^1/_2$ teaspoon salt
1 cup skim milk
$1^1/_2$ teaspoons ground cinnamon

Beat margarine and stevia blend until fluffy in medium bowl. Beat in egg, sour cream, and maple flavoring. In a separate bowl, combine flour, baking powder, and salt. Alternating with milk, beat flour mixture into margarine mixture. Spread $^1/_3$ of the batter into a greased and floured bundt pan. Sprinkle with $^1/_2$ of the cinnamon. Repeat layers, ending with cake batter. Bake cake in preheated 375°F oven for 25–30 minutes or till toothpick inserted in center of cake comes out clean. Cool cake in the pan for 5 minutes; remove from pan and cool on wire rack.

Makes 8 servings

NUTRITIONAL DATA (PER SERVING): 223 CALORIES; 8G TOTAL FAT; 5G PROTEIN; 32G CARBO-HYDRATE • FOOD EXCHANGES: 2 STARCH; $1^1/_2$ FAT

Chocolate Raspberry Cake

SURE TO BE A FAMILY FAVORITE.

4 teaspoons margarine, softened
¹/₄ cup raspberry spreadable fruit
1 each egg
5 teaspoons stevia blend
   or ⁵/₈ tsp. stevioside
   or 10 packets of stevia
3 teaspoons Dutch cocoa

1 ounce unsweetened baking
   chocolate
¹/₂ cup milk
1 cup flour
1 teaspoon baking powder
¹/₂ teaspoon baking soda
¹/₄ teaspoon salt

In a double boiler, combine Dutch cocoa, baking chocolate, and milk. Over medium heat, stir until smooth.

Beat margarine, preserves, egg, and stevia in medium bowl till smooth. In another bowl, combine flour, baking powder, baking soda, and salt. Mix dry ingredients into preserve mixture alternately with melted chocolate mixture. Pour batter into greased and floured, 8-inch cake pan. Bake in 350°F oven until toothpick inserted in center of cake comes out clean (about 20 minutes). Cool in pan 5 minutes; remove from pan and cool completely.

Makes 8 servings.

NUTRITIONAL DATA (PER SERVING): 130 CALORIES; 5G TOTAL FAT; 3G PROTEIN; 19G CARBO-HYDRATE • FOOD EXCHANGES: 1 STARCH; ¹/₂ FRUIT; 1 FAT

Dark Chocolate Bar Cake

A CHOCOHOLIC'S DREAM!

6 tablespoons margarine
5 ¹/₂ tablespoons stevia blend
  or ¹¹/₁₆ tsp. stevioside
  or 33 packets of stevia
4 ounces unsweetened chocolate
¹/₃ cup skim milk
¹/₃ cup apricot sugar-free
  preserves

3 each egg whites
¹/₈ teaspoon cream of tartar
¹/₄ cup flour
¹/₈ teaspoon salt
1 each egg yolk
1 teaspoon vanilla
Chocolate Glaze (optional, see
  index)

Heat margarine, chocolate, milk, and apricot preserves, in small saucepan, stirring frequently, until chocolate is almost melted. Remove pan from heat; continue stirring until chocolate is melted and mixture is smooth. Briskly stir in egg yolk, vanilla, and stevia.

Beat egg whites and cream of tartar to stiff peaks in large bowl. Fold chocolate mixture into egg whites. Combine flour and salt and fold into egg whites. Lightly grease bottom of 9-inch, round cake pan and line with wax paper. Pour cake batter into pan. Bake in preheated 350°F oven for 18–20 minutes till cake is just firm when lightly touched. (Do not over bake). Using a sharp knife, loosen the sides of the cake from the pan. This will help keep cake from cracking as it cools. Cool cake completely in pan on wire rack; refrigerate until chilled (1 to 2 hours). Remove cake from pan, and place on serving plate. Spread with Chocolate Glaze, if desired.

Makes 12 servings.

NUTRITIONAL DATA (PER SERVING): 150 CALORIES; 12G TOTAL FAT; 3G PROTEIN; 9G CARBO-HYDRATE • FOOD EXCHANGES: ¹/₂ STARCH; ¹/₂ LEAN MEAT; ¹/₂ FRUIT; 2¹/₂ FAT

Moist and Lite Chocolate Cupcakes

LOW-FAT CHOCOLATE TREATS.

1 cup flour
5 teaspoons stevia blend
  or ⁵/₈ tsp. stevioside
  or 10 packets of stevia
2 tablespoons cocoa

1 teaspoon baking soda
1 teaspoon baking powder
¹/₂ cup light salad dressing
¹/₂ cup water
1 teaspoon vanilla

In a large bowl, combine flour, stevia, cocoa, and baking soda. In a small bowl, stir together salad dressing, water, and vanilla until moist. Stir wet ingredients into dry ingredients until just mixed. Spoon into medium, greased muffin cups. Bake in 350°F oven for 12 minutes or until toothpick inserted in center comes out clean.

Makes 9 medium cupcakes.

NUTRITIONAL DATA (PER SERVING): 58 CALORIES; TRACE TOTAL FAT; 2G PROTEIN; 12G CARBOHYDRATE • FOOD EXCHANGES: 1 STARCH

Chocolate Cheesecake

Graham Cracker Crust:
1 1/4 cups graham cracker crumbs
4 tablespoons margarine, melted
1 teaspoon stevia blend
 or 1/8 tsp. stevioside
 or 2 packets of stevia
or Pretzel Crust (see index)

Cheesecake:
3 8-oz. packages cream cheese,
 softened
8 1/2 teaspoons stevia blend
 or 1 tsp. stevioside
 or 17 packets of stevia
3 each eggs
2 tablespoons cornstarch
1 cup sour cream
1/3 cup Dutch-process cocoa
1 teaspoon vanilla

Crust:

Mix graham cracker crumbs, margarine, and stevia in bottom of 9-inch springform pan. Pat graham cracker mixture evenly on bottom and 1/2 inch up side of pan.

Cheesecake:

Beat cream cheese and stevia in large bowl until fluffy; beat in eggs, and cornstarch. Mix in sour cream, cocoa, and vanilla until well blended. Pour mixture onto crust.

Place cheesecake in roasting pan on oven rack; add 1 inch of water to roasting pan. Bake cheesecake at 300°F for 45 to 50 minutes; just until set in the center. Turn oven off; remove cheesecake from roasting pan; return cheesecake to oven and let cheesecake cool 3 hours in oven with door slightly open. Refrigerate at least 8 hours. Remove cheesecake from pan. Place on serving plate.

Makes 16 servings.

NUTRITIONAL DATA (PER SERVING): 254 CALORIES; 23G TOTAL FAT; 6G PROTEIN; 9G CARBOHYDRATE • FOOD EXCHANGES: 1/2 STARCH; 1/2 LEAN MEAT; 4 FAT

New York Style Cheesecake

12 teaspoons stevia blend
  or 1 ½ tsp. stevioside
  or 24 packets of stevia
2 each eggs
2 each egg whites
2 tablespoons cornstarch

3 8-oz. packages cream cheese,
  softened
1 cup sour cream
1 teaspoon vanilla
Pretzel Crust (see index)

In a bowl, beat cream cheese and stevia until fluffy. Beat in egg whites, eggs, and cornstarch. Beat in vanilla and sour cream. Pour mixture over crust in a springform pan. Bake in a preheated oven at 300°F until firm in center (approx. 45–60 minutes). Turn off oven and let cheesecake cool. Refrigerate overnight. Serve with fresh fruit or a sauce if desired (see *Desert Sauces*).

Makes 16 servings.

NUTRITIONAL DATA (PER SERVING): 260 CALORIES; 25G TOTAL FAT; 7G PROTEIN; 4G CARBO-HYDRATE • FOOD EXCHANGES: 1 LEAN MEAT; 4½ FAT

Pumpkin Cheesecake
With Sour Cream Topping

24 ounces cream cheese

3 teaspoons stevia blend
   or $^3/_8$ tsp. stevioside
   or 6 packets of stevia

2 each eggs

15 ounces pumpkin

$^2/_3$ cup evaporated milk

2 tablespoons cornstarch

1 $^1/_4$ teaspoons ground cinnamon

$^1/_2$ teaspoon nutmeg

Topping:

2 cups sour cream

2 teaspoons stevia blend
   or $^1/_4$ tsp. stevioside
   or 4 packets of stevia

1 teaspoon vanilla

Pretzel Crust (see index)

Beat cream cheese and stevia in a large bowl until fluffy. Beat in eggs, pumpkin, and evaporated milk. Add cornstarch and spices. Beat well, and pour into crust. Bake at 350°F for 55 to 60 minutes until center is set.

Topping:

Combine sour cream, stevia blend, and vanilla in a bowl and mix well.

Spread topping over surface of warm cheesecake and allow to cool on a wire rack. Chill for several hours or overnight.

Makes 16 servings.

NUTRITIONAL DATA (PER SERVING): 247 CALORIES; 22G TOTAL FAT; 6G PROTEIN; 7G CARBO-HYDRATE • FOOD EXCHANGES: $^1/_2$ LEAN MEAT; $^1/_2$ VEGETABLE; 0 FRUIT; 4 FAT

CHAPTER 11

Pies & Pastries

PIES & PASTRIES

Apple Pie

6–8 each tart apples, peeled and
thinly sliced
3 teaspoons stevia blend
or ³/₈ tsp. stevioside
or 6 packets of stevia
3 tablespoons all-purpose flour

1 tablespoon cinnamon
1 dash ground nutmeg
2 tablespoons butter
1 tablespoon lemon juice
1 dash salt
Double-Crust Pastry (see index)

In a mixing bowl, combine stevia blend, lemon juice, flour, and spices.
Add apples; toss to coat fruit. Prepare Double-Crust Pastry. Place
bottom pastry in a 9-inch pie plate. Place apple pie filling in pastry.
Carefully position top crust. Seal and flute edge. Cover edge with foil.
Bake in a 375°F oven for 25 minutes. Remove foil. Bake for 20 to 25
minutes more till the top is golden and fruit is tender.

Serves 8.

NUTRITIONAL DATA (PER SERVING): 201 CALORIES; 9G TOTAL FAT; 2G PROTEIN; 29G CARBO-
HYDRATE • FOOD EXCHANGES: 1 STARCH; 1 FRUIT; 2 FAT

Cherry Pie

2 16-oz packages frozen, no-
 sugar-added, pitted cherries
³/₄ cup reserved cherry juice
5 tablespoons stevia blend
 or 1 ³/₄ tsp. stevioside
 or 30 packets of stevia

4 teaspoons all-purpose flour
4 teaspoons cornstarch
¹/₄ teaspoon ground nutmeg
1 teaspoon almond extract
Double-Crust Pastry (see index)

Thaw cherries completely in a strainer placed in a bowl; reserve 3/4 cup cherry juice. Set aside. In small, heavy saucepan, mix stevia, flour, cornstarch, and nutmeg. Stirring constantly, add cherry juice and heat to boiling. Continue stirring and cooking 2 more minutes. Remove from heat; stir in cherries and almond extract. Roll half of pastry on floured surface into circle 1 inch larger than inverted 9-inch pie pan. Place pastry into pan. Pour cherry mixture into pastry. Roll remaining pastry on floured surface to ¹/₈-inch thickness. Cut into 10 strips, ¹/₂-inch wide. Arrange pastry strips over filling. Weave into lattice design; trim. Fold edge of lower crust over ends of lattice strips. Seal and flute edge. Bake at 425°F for 35 to 40 minutes or till pastry is browned. Cool.

Makes 8 servings.

NUTRITIONAL DATA (PER SERVING): 163 CALORIES; 7G TOTAL FAT; 3G PROTEIN; 25G CARBO-HYDRATE • FOOD EXCHANGES: 1 STARCH; 1 FRUIT; 1 FAT

Vanilla Cream Pie

9 teaspoons stevia blend
   or 1 1/8 tsp. stevioside
   or 18 packets of stevia
1/4 cup cornstarch
2 tablespoons butter
3 cups milk

4 each egg yolks, beaten
2 teaspoons vanilla
baked Single-Crust Pastry (see index)
Meringue for Pie or Whipped Cream (see index)

Combine stevia, cornstarch, and milk in a saucepan. Stirring constantly, cook over medium heat till mixture is thick and bubbly. Reduce heat, add 1 tablespoon butter, and continue cooking and stirring for 3 more minutes. Stir 1 cup of hot mixture into beaten egg yolks. Stirring constantly, add all of egg mixture to the hot mixture in the saucepan. Still stirring constantly, cook over medium heat till near boiling. Continue cooking and stirring for 3 more minutes. Remove from heat. Stir in butter and vanilla. Pour the hot filling into baked crust.

Makes 8 servings.

NUTRITIONAL DATA (PER SERVING): 230 CALORIES; 15G TOTAL FAT; 6G PROTEIN; 18G CARBOHYDRATE • FOOD EXCHANGES: 1 STARCH; 2 1/2 FAT

Variations:

Banana Cream Pie: Prepare as above, but slice 2 medium bananas into the bottom of the baked crust. Pour filling over bananas.

Whipped Cream Topping: Prepare as above, chill hot pie, and then spread whipped cream over filling.

Meringue Topping: Prepare as above, but spread meringue over hot filling, sealing edges. Bake at 350°F for 15 minutes or till golden. Cool.

Chocolate Cream Pie

11 teaspoons stevia blend
   or 1 1/2 tsp. stevioside
   or 22 packets of stevia
1/4 cup cornstarch
3 ounces unsweetened chocolate,
   chopped
3 cups milk

4 each egg yolks, beaten
2 teaspoons vanilla
baked Single-Crust Pastry (see
   index)
Meringue or Whipped Cream (see
   index)

Combine stevia, cornstarch, and milk in a saucepan; add chopped chocolate. Stirring constantly, cook over medium heat till mixture is thick and bubbly. Reduce heat. Add 1 tablespoon butter; continue cooking and stirring for 3 more minutes. Stir 1 cup of hot mixture into beaten egg yolks. Stirring constantly, add all of egg mixture to the hot mixture in the saucepan. Cook over medium heat, still stirring constantly, till near boiling. Continue cooking and stirring for 3 more minutes. Remove from heat. Stir in butter and vanilla. Pour the hot filling into baked crust.

Makes 8 servings.

NUTRITIONAL DATA (PER SERVING): 260 CALORIES; 18G TOTAL FAT; 7G PROTEIN; 21G CARBOHYDRATE • FOOD EXCHANGES: 1 STARCH; 3 1/2 FAT

Variations:

Whipped Cream Topping: Chill hot pie then spread whipped cream over filling.

Meringue Topping: Prepare as above, but spread meringue over hot filling, sealing edges. Bake at 350°F for 15 minutes or till golden. Cool.

Nutty Coconut Cream Pie

9 teaspoons stevia blend
  or 1 ¹/₈ tsp. stevioside
  or 18 packets of stevia
¹/₃ cup cornstarch
2 tablespoons all-purpose flour
¹/₄ teaspoon salt
3 each eggs
3 cups milk
1 tablespoon butter
2 teaspoons vanilla extract

2 teaspoons almond extract
1 ¹/₄ cups coconut flakes (sugar-
  free coconut is available at
  health food stores)
³/₄ cup chopped toasted almonds
Whipped Cream (see index)
toasted coconut (optional)
prepared Coconut Crust (see
  index) or favorite single crust
  pastry

In medium saucepan, stir together stevia, cornstarch, flour, and salt; stir in eggs until mixture is well blended. Gradually stir in milk. Cook over medium heat, stirring constantly, until mixture boils; continue boiling and stirring 2 more minutes. Remove from heat. Stir in butter, almond extract and vanilla; stir in coconut and chopped almonds until blended. Pour into baked pie crust. Press plastic wrap directly onto surface; refrigerate 6 to 8 hours or until set. Just before serving, spread with Whipped Cream; sprinkle with toasted coconut.

Makes 8 servings.

NUTRITIONAL DATA (PER SERVING): 348 CALORIES; 23G TOTAL FAT; 10G PROTEIN; 26G CARBOHYDRATE • FOOD EXCHANGES: 1 ¹/₂ STARCH; ¹/₂ LEAN MEAT; 4 FAT

Coconut Custard Pie

THIS BAKED PIE IS FAST AND EASY TO PREPARE.

4 each eggs
1/4 teaspoon salt
2 cups skim milk
8 teaspoons stevia blend
   or 1 tsp. stevioside
   or 16 packets of stevia

2 teaspoons coconut extract
1/2 cup flaked coconut (or use
   sugar-free coconut meal,
   available at health food stores)
Single-Crust Pastry (see index)

Beat eggs and salt in large bowl until thick and lemon-colored (about 5 minutes). Mix in milk and remaining ingredients. Pour mixture into pastry. Bake pie in preheated 425°F oven for 15 minutes. Reduce temperature to 350°F and bake 20–25 more minutes or till a knife inserted near center comes out clean. Refrigerate till chilled (about 2 hours).

Makes 8 servings.

NUTRITIONAL DATA (PER SERVING): 172 CALORIES; 10G TOTAL FAT; 6G PROTEIN; 14G CARBOHYDRATE • FOOD EXCHANGES: 1/2 STARCH; 1/2 LEAN MEAT; 2 FAT

Lemon Meringue Pie

2 cups water
$^1/_4$ cup lemon juice
1 teaspoon lemon flavoring
7 teaspoons stevia blend
  or $^7/_8$ tsp. stevioside
  or 14 packets of stevia

5 tablespoons cornstarch
3 each eggs, beaten
1 teaspoon margarine
baked Single-Crust Pastry (see index)
Meringue (see index)

Mix water, lemon juice, stevia blend, and cornstarch in medium saucepan. Stirring constantly, heat to boiling; continue boiling and stirring 1 minute longer. Stir about 1 cup hot cornstarch mixture into the beaten eggs. Stirring constantly, add egg mixture to remaining hot cornstarch mixture; cook, still stirring constantly, over low heat for 5 minutes. Remove from heat; add margarine, stirring until melted. Pour mixture into baked pie shell.

Makes 8 servings.

NUTRITIONAL DATA (PER SERVING): 151 CALORIES; 8G TOTAL FAT; 3G PROTEIN; 16G CARBO-HYDRATE • FOOD EXCHANGES: 1 STARCH; $^1/_2$ LEAN MEAT; 1$^1/_2$ FAT

Key Lime Pie

1 envelope unflavored gelatin
1³/₄ cups milk
1 package (8 oz) cream cheese,
    softened
¹/₃ cup fresh lime juice

6 teaspoons stevia blend
    or ³/₄ tsp. stevioside
    or 12 packets of stevia
baked 9-inch Cookie Crust (see
    index)

Sprinkle gelatin over ¹/₂ cup milk in small saucepan; let stand 2 to 3 minutes to soften. Stirring constantly, cook over low heat, until gelatin is dissolved. In a small bowl, beat cream cheese until fluffy; beat in remaining 1¹/₄ cups milk and gelatin mixture. Mix in lime juice and stevia. Poor filling into cooled crust. Refrigerate pie until set (about 2 hours).

Makes 8 servings.

NUTRITIONAL DATA (PER SERVING): 238 CALORIES; 18G TOTAL FAT; 6G PROTEIN; 14G CARBOHYDRATE • FOOD EXCHANGES: ¹/₂ STARCH; ¹/₂ LEAN MEAT; 3¹/₂ FAT

Strawberry Cream Cheese Pie

1 8 oz. package cream cheese,
  softened
1 teaspoon vanilla
3 teaspoons stevia blend
  or ³/₈ tsp. stevioside
1 cup cold water
2 tablespoons cornstarch

1 package gelatin
6 teaspoons stevia blend
  or ³/₄ tsp. stevioside
  or 12 packets of stevia
1 pint strawberries, hulled, sliced
baked 9-inch Cookie Crust (see
  index)

Beat cream cheese, vanilla, and stevia in small bowl until fluffy; spread evenly in bottom of cooled crust. In small saucepan, mix cold water, 6 teaspoons stevia blend, and cornstarch; heat to boiling stirring constantly until thickened (about 2 minutes). Add gelatin, stirring until gelatin is dissolved. Cool 10 minutes. Arrange half of the sliced strawberries over the cream cheese. Spoon half the gelatin mixture over strawberries. Arrange remaining strawberries over pie and spoon remaining gelatin mixture over top. Refrigerate at least 2 hours or until pie is set and chilled.

Makes 8 servings.

NUTRITIONAL DATA (PER SERVING): 222 CALORIES; 16G TOTAL FAT; 4G PROTEIN; 15G CARBOHYDRATE • FOOD EXCHANGES: 1 STARCH; ¹/₂ LEAN MEAT; 3 FAT

Strawberry Chiffon Pie

2 1/2 cups fresh strawberries,
   hulled
6 teaspoons stevia blend
   or 1/2 tsp. stevioside
   or 12 packets of stevia
1 tablespoon lemon juice
1 envelope unflavored gelatin

2/3 cup water
2 each egg whites
1/2 cup whipping cream
Cookie Crust (see index)
Whipped Cream, optional (see
   index)

Crush strawberries with a fork in a large mixing bowl. Stir in 2 teaspoons stevia blend *or* 1/2 teaspoon stevioside and lemon juice; set aside.

Stir together 2 teaspoons stevia blend *or* 1/2 teaspoon stevioside, 2/3 cup water, and the gelatin in a small saucepan. Allow to soften 2 minutes. Cook over low heat, stirring constantly, till gelatin dissolves. Remove from heat. Cool to room temperature. Pour the cooled gelatin mixture into the strawberry mixture. Mix well. Refrigerate to the consistency of corn syrup, stirring occasionally (about 1 hour). Do not overchill. Remove from refrigerator.

In a large bowl, beat the egg whites on high speed with an electric mixer till soft peaks form. Gradually add 2 teaspoons stevia blend *or* 1/2 teaspoon stevioside. Beat till stiff peaks form. Fold in chilled gelatin mixture. In a medium bowl, beat cream till soft peaks form. Fold whipped cream into strawberry mixture. Chill about 1 hour. Spoon filling into cooled Cookie Crust. Chill pie at least 6 hours or till set.

Makes 8 servings.

NUTRITIONAL DATA (PER SERVING): 173 CALORIES; 12G TOTAL FAT; 4G PROTEIN; 14G CARBOHYDRATE • FOOD EXCHANGES: 1/2 STARCH; 2 1/2 FAT

Sour Cream and Raisin Pie

9 teaspoons stevia blend
   or 1 ¹/₈ tsp. stevioside
   or 18 packets of stevia
¹/₃ cup cornstarch
3 cups milk
4 each egg yolks, beaten
1 tablespoon butter

2 teaspoons vanilla
1 cup raisins
¹/₂ cup sour cream
baked Single-Crust Pastry (see index)
Whipped Cream (see index)

Combine stevia, cornstarch, and milk in a saucepan. Stirring continuously, cook over medium heat till mixture is thick and bubbly. Reduce heat; continue cooking and stirring for 3 more minutes. Stir 1 cup of hot mixture into beaten egg yolks. Stirring constantly, add all of egg mixture to the hot mixture in the saucepan. Cook, stirring constantly, over medium heat till near boiling. Continue cooking and stirring for 3 more minutes. Remove from heat. Stir in raisins, sour cream, butter, and vanilla. Pour the hot filling into baked crust. Chill. Spread whipped cream over pie. Serve cold.

Makes 8 servings.

NUTRITIONAL DATA (PER SERVING): 307 CALORIES; 16G TOTAL FAT; 7G PROTEIN; 35G CARBOHYDRATE • FOOD EXCHANGES: 1 STARCH; 1 FRUIT; 3 FAT

Pumpkin Pie

GUESTS WILL NEVER KNOW WHAT'S MISSING.

5 teaspoons stevia blend
   or ⁵/₈ tsp. stevioside
   or 10 packets of stevia
¹/₂ teaspoon salt
1 teaspoon ground cinnamon
¹/₂ teaspoon ginger

1/4 teaspoon allspice
2 each eggs
15 ounces pumpkin pie filling
1 ¹/₂ cups evaporated milk
Single-Crust Pastry(see index)

In a large bowl, combine all ingredients. Mix until fluffy. Pour into pie crust. Bake at 350°F for 40 to 50 minutes or until a knife inserted into the center comes out clean. Allow to cool. Top with Whipped Cream (see index).

Makes 8 servings.

NUTRITIONAL DATA (PER SERVING): 199 CALORIES; 11G TOTAL FAT; 7G PROTEIN; 20G CARBOHYDRATE • FOOD EXCHANGES: ¹/₂ STARCH; 1 VEGETABLE; 0 FRUIT; 2 FAT

Meringue for Pie

4 each egg whites
$^1/_4$ teaspoon cream of tartar
$^1/_2$ teaspoon vanilla

3 teaspoons stevia blend
or $^3/_8$ tsp. stevioside
or 6 packets of stevia

Beat 4 egg whites and vanilla in medium bowl until foamy; add cream of tartar and beat to soft peaks. Gradually beat in 3 teaspoons stevia blend, beating to stiff peaks. Spread meringue over pie, carefully sealing edge of crust. Bake in a 350°F oven for 15 minutes or till golden.

Makes 8 servings.

NUTRITIONAL DATA (PER SERVING): 9 CALORIES; 0G TOTAL FAT; 2G PROTEIN; TRACE CARBOHYDRATE • FOOD EXCHANGES: FREE

Double-Crust Pastry

2 cups all-purpose flour
$^1/_2$ teaspoon salt
$^2/_3$ cup shortening
2 teaspoons stevia blend

or $^1/_4$ tsp. stevioside
or 4 packets of stevia
6–7 tablespoons water

Stir together flour, stevia, and salt in a mixing bowl. Cut in shortening till pieces are the size of small peas. Slowly add water, 1 tablespoon at a time, till dough is moist. Divide dough in half. Form each half into a ball. On a floured surface, flatten one ball of dough. Roll dough to form a circle about 1 inch larger than an inverted 9-inch pie plate. Wrap pastry around rolling pin. Unroll into a 9-inch pie plate. For top crust, roll remaining dough. Cut slits to let steam out.

Fill crust in pie plate with filling. Place top crust on filling. Trim crust $^1/_2$ inch beyond plate. Flute edge. Bake as directed in individual recipes.

NUTRITIONAL DATA (PER WHOLE): 2118 CALORIES; 139G TOTAL FAT; 26G PROTEIN; 191G CARBOHYDRATE • FOOD EXCHANGES: 12$^1/_2$ STARCH; 27$^1/_2$ FAT

Variation:

Cheese Pastry: Prepare as above, adding 1 cup shredded cheddar cheese to flour. Perfect for apple pie.

Single-Crust Pastry

1 1/4 cups all-purpose flour
1/4 teaspoon salt
1/3 cup shortening
3–4 tablespoons water

2 teaspoons stevia blend
or 1/4 tsp. stevioside
or 4 packets of stevia

Stir together flour, stevia, and salt in a mixing bowl. Cut in shortening till pieces are the size of small peas. Slowly add water, 1 tablespoon at a time, till dough is moist. Form into a ball. On a floured surface, flatten one ball of dough. Roll dough to form a circle about 1 inch larger than an inverted 9-inch pie plate. Wrap pastry around rolling pin. Unroll into a 9-inch pie plate. Trim to 1/2 inch beyond edge of pie plate; fold crust under. Flute edges. Bake as directed in recipes.

Baked Pastry Shell: Prepare as above; with a fork, prick bottom and sides of pastry. Bake at 450°F for 10 to 14 minutes or till golden. Cool.

NUTRITIONAL DATA (PER WHOLE): 1173 CALORIES; 70G TOTAL FAT; 16G PROTEIN; 119G CARBOHYDRATE • FOOD EXCHANGES: 8 STARCH; 13 1/2 FAT

Oil Pastry

THIS LIGHT AND FLAKY CRUST IS EASY TO MAKE.

$^1/_2$ cup milk
$^1/_2$ cup cooking oil
2 teaspoons stevia blend
  or 1/4 tsp. stevioside

or 4 packets of stevia
2 cups flour
salt to taste

In a mixing bowl, stir together flour and salt. Pour oil and milk into a measuring cup; add all at once to flour mixture. Stir with a fork. Form into 2 balls. Place each ball of dough between 2 squares of wax paper. Roll each ball into a circle. Peel off top paper and fit dough, paper side up, into 9-inch pie plates. Remove paper.

Makes one 9-inch double-crust pastry or two 9-inch single-crust pastries.

NUTRITIONAL DATA (PER WHOLE): 1949 CALORIES; 116G TOTAL FAT; 30G PROTEIN; 196G CARBOHYDRATE • FOOD EXCHANGES: 12$^1/_2$ STARCH; 22$^1/_2$ FAT

Rich Pastry

³/₄ cup all-purpose flour
3 teaspoons stevia blend
   or ³/₈ tsp. stevioside
   or 6 packets of stevia
2¹/₄ teaspoons cornstarch

¹/₈ teaspoon salt
6 tablespoons margarine, cut into
   pieces
³/₄ teaspoon vanilla

Combine flour, stevia blend, cornstarch, and salt in medium bowl; cut in margarine until mixture resembles coarse crumbs. Sprinkle with vanilla; mix with hands to form dough. Press dough evenly on bottom and ¹/₄-inch up side of 8-inch, square baking pan. Bake in preheated 350°F oven until lightly browned (about 10 minutes). Cool on wire rack.

Makes 16 servings.

NUTRITIONAL DATA (PER WHOLE): 983 CALORIES; 69G TOTAL FAT; 10G PROTEIN; 79G CARBOHYDRATE • FOOD EXCHANGES: 5 STARCH; 13¹/₂ FAT

Cookie Crust

½ cup butter
3 ounces cream cheese
2 cups flour
2 tablespoons stevia blend
  or ¼ tsp. stevioside

or 12 packets of stevia
1 each egg
½ teaspoon baking powder
½ teaspoon vanilla

In a medium bowl, beat margarine, cream cheese, and stevia with an electric mixer on high speed till creamy. Add 1 cup of the flour, egg, baking powder, and vanilla. Beat till well blended. Mix in remaining flour. Cover; chill 1 hour. Roll into circle on wax paper. Invert over pie pan; shape edge. Bake in a 375°F oven about 12 minutes or till golden. Cool before filling. Use for chiffon, pudding, or ice-cream pies.

Makes one 9-inch, single-crust pastry.

NUTRITIONAL DATA (PER WHOLE): 2093 CALORIES; 128G TOTAL FAT; 39G PROTEIN; 195G CARBOHYDRATE • FOOD EXCHANGES: 12½ STARCH; 1½ LEAN MEAT; 24½ FAT

Variations:

Chocolate Cookie Crust: Prepare as above, increasing stevia blend to 2½ tablespoons and adding 2 squares (2 ounces) unsweetened chocolate, melted and slightly cooled, with the butter and cream cheese mixture.

Orange Cookie Crust: Prepare as above, adding ½ teaspoon orange zest and 1 tablespoon frozen orange juice concentrate with the vanilla.

Coconut Crust

2 cups flaked coconut
2 teaspoons stevia blend
  or ¼ tsp. stevioside

or 4 packets of stevia
3 tablespoons margarine or butter, melted

In a bowl, mix 2 cups flaked coconut with stevia. Next, add melted margarine or butter. Press firmly onto bottom and sides of a 9-inch pie plate. Bake in a 325°F oven for 20 minutes or till edge is golden. Cool before filling. Great for chiffon, ice-cream, or coconut pies.

NUTRITIONAL DATA (PER WHOLE): 871 CALORIES; 88G TOTAL FAT; 6G PROTEIN; 25G CARBO-HYDRATE • FOOD EXCHANGES: 1½ FRUIT; 17½ FAT

Grape-Nuts® Crust

1½ cups Grape-Nuts[a]
4 tablespoons margarine or butter
2 teaspoons stevia blend

or ¼ tsp. stevioside
or 4 packets of stevia
½ teaspoon salt

Melt margarine and mix with **Grape-Nuts®**. Sprinkle stevia blend and salt over the mixture and mix well. Pack into a baking dish that will be used to bake the pie or cheesecake. Place in a preheated oven at 350°F for 8 minutes or until crust in lightly browned. Allow to cool before using with cheesecake or pie.

NUTRITIONAL DATA (PER WHOLE): 1015 CALORIES; 48G TOTAL FAT; 20G PROTEIN; 140G CARBOHYDRATE • FOOD EXCHANGES: 9 STARCH; 9½ FAT

Pretzel Crust

1 1/2 cups pretzels, crushed
4 tablespoons margarine or butter
2 teaspoons stevia blend

or 1/4 tsp. stevioside
or 4 packets of stevia

Melt margarine and mix with crushed pretzels. Sprinkle stevia over the mixture and mix well. Pack into a baking dish that will be used to bake the pie or cheesecake. Place in a preheated oven at 350°F for 8 minutes or until crust is lightly browned. Allow to cool before using with cheesecake or pie.

NUTRITIONAL DATA (PER WHOLE): 1758 CALORIES; 58G TOTAL FAT; 32G PROTEIN; 281G CARBOHYDRATE • FOOD EXCHANGES: 17 1/2 STARCH; 11 1/2 FAT

CHAPTER 12

Desserts & Candies

DESSERTS & CANDIES

Almond Velvet Ice Cream – 200
Baked Apples – 192
Bread Pudding – 186
Cappuccino Ice Cream – 199
Chocolate Chips – 209
Chocolate Chocolate-Chip Ice Cream – 198
Chocolate Fudge Treats – 208
Chocolate Ice Cream – 198
Chocolate Mousse – 188
Chocolate Pudding – 187
Cream Puffs – 205
Creamy Frozen Pops – 203
Creamy Stirred Rice Pudding – 189
Dessert Crepes – 204
Dipping Chocolate – 209
Flan with Butterscotch Sauce – 191
Fresh Fruit Yogurt – 195
Fruit Juice Gelatin Blocks – 194
Fruity Gelatin – 195
Fudge Balls – 207
Light & Fluffy Tapioca – 190
Orange Frozen Yogurt – 201
Peach Cobbler – 193
Peanut Butter Balls – 206
Pina Colada Frozen Yogurt – 202
Poached Pears – 194
Powdered Sugar Replacement – 210
Sour Cream Vanilla Pudding – 185
Vanilla Ice Cream – 196
Vanilla Ice Milk – 197
Vanilla Pudding – 185
Yogurt with Fruit Preserves – 196

Vanilla Pudding

6 teaspoons stevia blend
  or ³/₄ tsp. stevioside
  or 12 packets of stevia
3 tablespoons cornstarch

3 cups milk
4 each eggs, beaten
1 tablespoon margarine
2 teaspoons vanilla

In a heavy medium saucepan, combine stevia blend and cornstarch. Stir in milk. Stirring constantly, cook over medium heat till mixture is thickened and bubbly. Continue cooking and stirring for 2 more minutes. Remove from heat. Gradually stir about 1 cup of the hot mixture into beaten eggs. Slowly stir all of the egg mixture into the remaining hot mixture in the saucepan. Cook till nearly bubbly, but do not boil. Reduce heat. Continue cooking and stirring 3 more minutes. Remove from heat. Stir in margarine and vanilla. Pour pudding into a bowl. Cover the surface with clear plastic wrap. Chill.

Makes 6 servings.

NUTRITIONAL DATA (PER SERVING): 155 CALORIES; 9G TOTAL FAT;8G PROTEIN; 10G CARBO-HYDRATE • FOOD EXCHANGES: ¹/₂ LEAN MEAT; 1 ¹/₂ FAT

Variation:

Sour Cream Vanilla Pudding: Prepare as above. After chilling, stir in one 8-ounce carton dairy sour cream.

Bread Pudding

TRY THIS CLASSIC DESSERT FOR BREAKFAST.

4 beaten eggs
2 cups milk
8 teaspoons stevia blend
   or 1 tsp. stevioside
   or 16 packets of stevia

1 teaspoon ground cinnamon
1 teaspoon vanilla
3 cups (4 slices) dry bread cubes
⅓ cup raisins, chopped

Place dry bread cubes in an 8 x 1½-inch baking dish. Sprinkle raisins over bread. In a medium mixing bowl, beat together eggs, milk, stevia, cinnamon, and vanilla. Pour egg mixture over the bread and raisins. Bake in a 325°F oven for 35–40 minutes or till a knife inserted near the center comes out clean. Cool slightly. Serve with Stirred Custard Sauce (see index).

Makes 6 servings.

NUTRITIONAL DATA (PER SERVING): 310 CALORIES; 9G TOTAL FAT; 13G PROTEIN; 44G CARBOHYDRATE • FOOD EXCHANGES: 2½ STARCH; ½ LEAN MEAT; 1½ FAT

Chocolate Pudding

9 teaspoons stevia blend
  or 1 tsp. stevioside
  or 18 packets of stevia
1/3 cup cocoa powder
3 tablespoons cornstarch

3 cups milk
4 each egg yolks
1 tablespoon margarine
2 teaspoons vanilla

In a heavy saucepan, combine stevia, cornstarch, and cocoa. Add milk; stir well. Over medium heat, stirring constantly, cook till mixture is thickened and bubbly. Continue cooking and stirring for 1 minute more. Remove from heat. Stir about 1 cup of the hot milk mixture into the beaten egg yolks. Add all of the egg mixture to the remaining hot milk mixture in the saucepan. Stirring constantly, cook till nearly boiling. Do not boil, or mixture may curdle. Reduce heat; continue cooking and stirring 3 minutes more. Remove from heat. Stir in margarine and vanilla. Pour pudding into a bowl. Cover the surface with clear plastic wrap. Chill in refrigerator at least 2 hours before serving.

Makes 4 Servings

NUTRITIONAL DATA (PER SERVING): 255 CALORIES; 15G TOTAL FAT; 10G PROTEIN; 20G CARBOHYDRATE • FOOD EXCHANGES: 1/2 STARCH; 1/2 LEAN MEAT; 2 1/2 FAT

Chocolate Mousse

1 teaspoon (1 pkg.) gelatin
1 tablespoon cold water
1 tablespoon boiling water
6 teaspoons stevia blend
   or ³/₄ tsp. stevioside

or 12 packets of stevia
¹/₄ cup cocoa powder
1 cup heavy whipping cream
1 teaspoon vanilla

In a small bowl, sprinkle gelatin over cold water; let stand 5 minutes to soften. Add boiling water, stirring until gelatin is completely dissolved and mixture is clear. Cool slightly. In medium bowl, stir together stevia and cocoa; add whipping cream and vanilla. Beat at medium speed, scraping bottom of bowl occasionally, until stiff peaks form. Pour in gelatin mixture and beat until well blended. Spoon into serving dishes. Chill about ¹/₂ hour.

Makes 4 servings.

NUTRITIONAL DATA (PER SERVING): 229 CALORIES; 23G TOTAL FAT; 4G PROTEIN; 4G CARBO-HYDRATE • FOOD EXCHANGES: ¹/₂ LEAN MEAT; 4¹/₂ FAT

Variations: Add a dash of rum, Kahlua or instant coffee crystals while beating mixture.

Creamy Stirred Rice Pudding

3 cups milk
$^1/_3$ cup long grain rice
$^1/_3$ cup chopped raisins
3$^1/_2$ teaspoons stevia blend

or $^7/_{16}$ tsp. stevioside
or 7 packets of stevia
1 teaspoon vanilla
$^1/_2$ teaspoon ground nutmeg

In a heavy, medium saucepan, bring milk to boiling. Stir in uncooked rice and raisins. Cover; cook over low heat, stirring often, for 30 to 40 minutes or till most of the milk is absorbed. (Mixture may appear lumpy.) Stir in the stevia blend, vanilla, and nutmeg. Spoon into dessert dishes. Serve warm or cold.

Makes 6 servings.

NUTRITIONAL DATA (PER SERVING): 140 CALORIES; 4G TOTAL FAT; 5G PROTEIN; 21G CARBO-HYDRATE • FOOD EXCHANGES: $^1/_2$ STARCH; $^1/_2$ FRUIT; $^1/_2$ FAT

Light & Fluffy Tapioca

---

1 each egg white
1 tablespoon nonfat dry milk
   powder
3 teaspoons stevia blend
   or ³/₈ tsp. stevioside

or 6 packets of stevia
3 tablespoons minute tapioca
2 cups milk
1 each egg yolk
1 ½ teaspoons vanilla

In a small bowl, mix 1 teaspoon stevia blend with 1 tablespoon of dry powdered milk; set aside. In another bowl, using an electric mixer on high speed, beat egg white until foamy. Gradually add powdered milk mixture to egg whites, beating until soft peaks form. Mix tapioca with remaining stevia blend, milk, and egg yolk in a medium saucepan. Let stand 5 minutes. Stirring constantly, cook on medium heat until mixture comes to a full boil. Remove from heat. Stir tapioca mixture into egg-white mixture until well blended. Stir in vanilla. Dispense into small dessert bowls. Cool.

Makes approximately 6 servings.

NUTRITIONAL DATA (PER SERVING): 87 CALORIES; 4G TOTAL FAT; 4G PROTEIN; 9G CARBOHY-DRATE • FOOD EXCHANGES: ½ STARCH; 0 FRUIT; ½ FAT

Flan with Butterscotch Sauce

1 quart skim milk
5 each eggs
7 teaspoons stevia blend
  or ⁷/₈ tsp. stevioside

or 14 packets of stevia
2 teaspoons vanilla
Butterscotch Sauce (see index)

In a heavy saucepan, heat milk just to simmering. Beat eggs until foamy in medium bowl; gradually whisk hot milk into eggs. Stir in stevia and vanilla. Pour milk mixture through a strainer into an ungreased, 1-quart casserole or soufflé dish; cover with lid or aluminum foil. Place dish in roasting pan on middle rack of oven. Pour 2 inches of water into roasting pan. Bake at 325°F until custard is set and sharp knife inserted near the center comes out clean (1 to 1¼ hours). Remove dish from roasting pan, and cool to room temperature on wire rack. Refrigerate until chilled (5 to 6 hours). Spoon custard into dishes; top with Butterscotch Sauce.

Makes 5 servings.

NUTRITIONAL DATA (PER SERVING): 139 CALORIES; 5G TOTAL FAT; 12G PROTEIN; 11G CARBOHYDRATE • FOOD EXCHANGES: 1 LEAN MEAT; ½ FAT

Baked Apples

4 each small apples
1 teaspoon butter or margarine
2 teaspoons stevia blend
  or $^1/_4$ tsp. stevioside
  or 4 packets of stevia

$^1/_3$ teaspoon cinnamon
$^1/_3$ cup apple juice or water
$^1/_2$ cup raisins or mixed dried fruit
  bits

Remove apple cores, leaving half an inch of core at bottom of each apple. Prick skins with fork; place apples in a 2-quart casserole. In a small saucepan, melt margarine. Stir in stevia, cinnamon, lemon juice, raisins, and walnuts. Spoon mixture into apple centers. Bake in a 350°F oven for 40 to 45 minutes or till apples are tender. Let stand a few minutes, and spoon liquid back into apples before serving.

Makes 4 servings.

NUTRITIONAL DATA (PER SERVING): 158 CALORIES; 2G TOTAL FAT; 1G PROTEIN; 39G CARBO-HYDRATE • FOOD EXCHANGES: 2$^1/_2$ FRUIT

Peach Cobbler

Filling:
3 15-oz cans sugar-free peaches,
 drained (reserve 1 cup liquid)
3 tablespoons cornstarch
2 teaspoons stevia blend
 or ¹/₄ tsp. stevioside
 or 4 packets of stevia
¹/₂ teaspoon cinnamon

Topping:
1 cup all-purpose flour
1 teaspoon stevia blend
 or ¹/₈ tsp. stevioside
 or 2 packets of stevia
1 teaspoon baking powder
¹/₂ teaspoon cinnamon
3 tablespoons butter
1 each egg
3 tablespoons buttermilk

Filling:

In a heavy saucepan, combine stevia and 3 tablespoons cornstarch.
Add 1 cup of reserved liquid. Stir till cornstarch is dissolved. Add 3
drained cans of peaches. Cook and stir till thick.

Topping:

In a medium bowl, mix flour, stevia, baking powder, and cinnamon.
Cut in butter till mixture resembles coarse crumbs. In a small bowl,
combine egg and milk. Add to flour mixture stirring till just moistened.
Transfer hot filling to an 8 x 8 x 2-inch baking dish. Drop topping into
6 mounds atop filling. Bake in a 400°F oven 20–25 minutes or till a
toothpick inserted into topping comes out clean. Serve warm.

NUTRITIONAL DATA (PER SERVING): 189 CALORIES; 4G TOTAL FAT; 3G PROTEIN; 38G CARBO-
HYDRATE • FOOD EXCHANGES: 1 STARCH; 1¹/₂ FRUIT; ¹/₂ FAT

Poached Pears

2 teaspoons stevia blend
  or ¹/₄ tsp. stevioside
  or 4 packets of stevia
1 cup orange juice

1 teaspoon cinnamon
1 teaspoon vanilla
4 each pears, peeled, halved, and
  cored

Bring stevia, orange juice, and vanilla to boiling in a large skillet. Add pears. Reduce heat, cover, and allow to simmer for 10 to 15 minutes or till tender. Serve warm or chilled.

Makes 4 servings.

NUTRITIONAL DATA (PER SERVING): 130 CALORIES; 1G TOTAL FAT; 1G PROTEIN; 32G CARBO-HYDRATE • FOOD EXCHANGES: 2 FRUIT

Fruit Juice Gelatin Blocks

4 envelopes unflavored gelatin
4 teaspoons stevia blend
  or ¹/₂ tsp. stevioside
  or 8 packets of stevia

1 cup cold fruit juice
3 cups fruit juice, heated to
  boiling

In a medium bowl, sprinkle gelatin over cold juice; let stand 2 minutes. Add hot juice and stir until dissolved. Pour into 13 x 9-inch baking pan; chill until set. Cut into 1-inch squares.

Makes about 12 blocks.

NUTRITIONAL DATA (PER SERVING): 86 CALORIES; TRACE PROTEIN; 0G TOTAL FAT • FOOD EXCHANGES: FREE

Fruity Gelatin

A GUILT-FREE TREAT WITH AS LITTLE AS 6 CALORIES PER SERVING.

2 envelopes unflavored gelatin   4 cups Stevia Punch, see index

In a saucepan, sprinkle gelatin over Stevia Punch. Allow to stand 3 minutes. Stirring constantly, heat mixture to a low boil over medium heat. Remove from heat; cool. Pour into desert cups. Chill till set. Makes 8 servings.

NUTRITIONAL DATA (PER SERVING): 12 CALORIES; 0G TOTAL FAT; 3G PROTEIN • FOOD EXCHANGES: ¹/₂ LEAN MEAT

Fresh Fruit Yogurt

FAST, EASY, AND SUGAR-FREE.

¹/₂ cup strawberries, sliced (or   *or* ³/₁₆ tsp. stevioside
   your favorite fruit)   *or* 3 packets of stevia
1 cup yogurt   ¹/₄ teaspoon strawberry flavoring,
1 ¹/₂ teaspoons stevia blend   optional

Combine all ingredients in bowl; mix well. Serve chilled. Makes 2 (6-ounce) servings.

Note: Any fruit can be used but, depending on the fruit, you may need to adjust the amount of stevia blend to personal taste.

NUTRITIONAL DATA (PER SERVING): 173 CALORIES; 8G TOTAL FAT; 9G PROTEIN; 17G CARBO-HYDRATE • FOOD EXCHANGES: ¹/₂ FRUIT; 1 ¹/₂ FAT; ¹/₂ OTHER CARBOHYDRATES

Yogurt with Fruit Preserves

THIS FAST, FRUIT YOGURT TASTES BETTER THAN COMMERCIAL BRANDS.

1 cup plain yogurt
2 tablespoons sugar-free fruit
   preserves

$^1/_2$ teaspoon stevia blend
   or $^1/_{16}$ tsp. stevioside
   or 1 packet of stevia

In a small bowl, combine all ingredients. Mix well. Serve chilled.

Makes 1 serving.

NUTRITIONAL DATA (PER SERVING): 222 CALORIES; 8G TOTAL FAT; 9G PROTEIN; 29G CARBO-HYDRATE • FOOD EXCHANGES: 1 FRUIT; 1$^1/_2$ FAT; $^1/_2$ OTHER CARBOHYDRATES

Vanilla Ice Cream

5 teaspoons stevia blend
   or $^5/_8$ tsp. stevioside
   or 10 packets of stevia
1 cup milk

1 pinch salt
1 cup half-and-half
2 cups whipping cream
1$^1/_2$ teaspoons vanilla extract

Scald milk, stirring constantly. Slowly add stevia until dissolved. Remove from heat and stir in salt, half-and-half, cream, and vanilla. Cover and refrigerate until cool. Freeze according to ice-cream maker manufacturer's instructions.

Makes 8 servings.

NUTRITIONAL DATA (PER SERVING): 266 CALORIES; 27G TOTAL FAT; 3G PROTEIN; 5G CARBO-HYDRATE • FOOD EXCHANGES: 5$^1/_2$ FAT

Vanilla Ice Milk

REQUIRES NO COOKING.

1 can (13-ounces) evaporated
  milk
7 1/2 teaspoons stevia blend
  or 7/8 tsp. stevioside

or 15 packets of stevia
1 1/2 cups whole milk
1 tablespoon vanilla
3 each eggs

Combine evaporated milk and stevia. Beat well until stevia is dissolved. Add whole milk and vanilla extract; beat well. Beat eggs into milk mixture vigorously. Pour into ice-cream maker. Freeze according to ice-cream maker manufacturer's directions.

Makes 6 servings.

NUTRITIONAL DATA (PER SERVING): 159 CALORIES; 9G TOTAL FAT; 9G PROTEIN; 10G CARBO-HYDRATE • FOOD EXCHANGES: 1/2 LEAN MEAT; 1 1/2 FAT

Chocolate Ice Cream

4 tablespoons stevia blend
  or $1/2$ tsp. stevioside
  or 24 packets of stevia
3 tablespoons cocoa powder
1 tablespoon cornstarch
$1/4$ teaspoon salt

3 cups milk
2 each eggs, beaten
$2/3$ cup half-and-half
1 cup whipping cream
1 teaspoon vanilla extract

Combine stevia, cocoa, cornstarch, and salt in a saucepan. Gradually stir in milk, and cook over medium heat, stirring constantly, until mixture begins to simmer. Gradually stir 1 cup of the hot mixture into the beaten eggs. Stirring constantly, gradually pour egg mixture into remaining hot milk mixture. Continue cooking and stirring over low heat until slightly thickened. Stir in half-and-half, whipping cream, and vanilla. Cover and refrigerate until cold. Freeze according to directions of ice-cream machine manufacturer.

NUTRITIONAL DATA (PER SERVING): 211 CALORIES; 18G TOTAL FAT; 6G PROTEIN; 8G CARBO-HYDRATE • FOOD EXCHANGES: $3^{1}/2$ FAT

Variation:

Chocolate Chocolate-Chip Ice Cream: For a bittersweet chocolate delight, take 1–2 ounces of Bakers unsweetened chocolate squares and melt them in a double boiler. Add stevia to the melted chocolate until desired sweetness is obtained. Allow to cool but not harden. Spread chocolate on wax paper; allow to harden. Remove paper; break chocolate into small pieces. Halfway through the processing of the ice cream, open the container and slowly stir in the chocolate. Close cover and resume processing of ice cream.

Cappuccino Ice Cream

4 tablespoons stevia blend
  or 1 1/2 tsp. stevioside
  or 24 packets of stevia
1 tablespoon instant coffee
  crystals
2 tablespoons cocoa powder
1 tablespoon cornstarch

1/4 teaspoon salt
3 cups milk
2 each eggs, beaten
2/3 cup half-and-half
1 cup whipping cream
1 teaspoon vanilla extract

In a small bowl, gently beat eggs; set aside. In a saucepan, combine stevia, instant coffee crystals, cocoa, cornstarch, and salt. Gradually stir in milk. Stirring constantly, cook over medium heat until mixture begins to simmer. Gradually stir 1 cup of the hot milk mixture into the beaten eggs. Gradually stir all of the egg mixture into the remaining hot milk mixture in the saucepan. Continue cooking and stirring over low heat until slightly thickened; then cook 2 more minutes. Stir in half-and-half, whipping cream, and vanilla. Cover and refrigerate until cold. Freeze according to directions of ice-cream machine manufacturer.

Makes 8 servings.

NUTRITIONAL DATA (PER SERVING): 212 CALORIES; 18G TOTAL FAT; 6G PROTEIN; 8G CARBO-HYDRATE • FOOD EXCHANGES: 3 1/2 FAT

Almond Velvet Ice Cream

**THIS NUTTY TREAT REQUIRES NO COOKING
AND NO ICE-CREAM MACHINE.**

2 cups whipping cream
1 cup evaporated milk
2 teaspoons stevia blend
  or ¼ tsp. stevioside

or 4 packets of stevia
1 teaspoon almond flavoring
⅓ cup almonds, coarsely chopped

Combine cream, condensed milk, stevia, and almond flavoring. Beat with an electric mixer till soft peaks form. Fold in chopped nuts. Transfer to an 8 x 8 x 2-inch pan; place in your freezer till firm. Makes 1 quart.

Makes 8 servings.

NUTRITIONAL DATA (PER SERVING): 283 CALORIES; 27G TOTAL FAT; 5G PROTEIN; 6G CARBO-
HYDRATE • FOOD EXCHANGES: 5½ FAT

Orange Frozen Yogurt

1 envelope unflavored gelatin
$^1/_2$ cup cold water
1 6-ounce can frozen orange juice
   concentrate, thawed
3 16-ounce cartons plain, low-fat
   yogurt, unsweetened

4$^1/_2$ tablespoons stevia blend
  or 1$^1/_2$ tsp. stevioside
  or 27 packets of stevia

In a small, heavy saucepan, combine gelatin and water. Let stand 5 minutes. Stirring constantly, heat until gelatin dissolves. Remove from heat. In a large mixing bowl, combine thawed orange juice concentrate, yogurt, stevia, and vanilla. Mix in gelatin mixture. Pour into a 4-quart ice-cream freezer; freeze according to ice-cream maker manufacturer's directions.

Makes about 8 servings.

NUTRITIONAL DATA (PER SERVING): 141 CALORIES; 6G TOTAL FAT; 7G PROTEIN; 16G CARBO-HYDRATE • FOOD EXCHANGES: $^1/_2$ FRUIT; 1 FAT; $^1/_2$ OTHER CARBOHYDRATES

Pina Colada Frozen Yogurt

THIS FROZEN TREAT REQUIRES NO COOKING.

$^1/_2$ teaspoon vanilla extract
4 teaspoons stevia blend
   or $^1/_2$ tsp. stevioside
   or 8 packets of stevia
$^3/_4$ teaspoon rum extract

4 cups plain yogurt, unsweetened
14 ounces crushed pineapple in
   juice
14 ounces coconut milk
$^1/_2$ cup whipping cream

Dissolve stevia into yogurt. Add remaining ingredients; mix well. Freeze according to ice-cream maker manufacturers instructions.

Makes 8 servings.

NUTRITIONAL DATA (PER SERVING): 258 CALORIES; 21G TOTAL FAT; 6G PROTEIN; 13G CARBOHYDRATE • FOOD EXCHANGES: $^1/_2$ FRUIT; 4 FAT; $^1/_2$ OTHER CARBOHYDRATES

Creamy Frozen Pops

1 can evaporated milk, chilled
4 teaspoons stevia blend
   or 1/2 tsp. stevioside
   or 8 packets of stevia

1 teaspoon vanilla
1 package gelatin
1/4 cup water

In a small saucepan, sprinkle gelatin over 1/4 cup cold water; let stand 5 minutes. Stir over low heat until gelatin is completely dissolved. Allow to cool to room temperature.

In a large bowl, combine cold evaporated milk, stevia, vanilla, and gelatin. With electric mixer, beat till soft peaks form. Spoon mixture into 3-ounce paper cups. Cover with foil. Insert wooden sticks through the foil into the mixture. Freeze till firm.

NUTRITIONAL DATA (PER SERVING): 75 CALORIES; 4G TOTAL FAT; 5G PROTEIN; 5G CARBOHYDRATE • FOOD EXCHANGES: 1/2 FAT

Dessert Crepes

1 ½ cups milk
1 cup all-purpose flour
2 each eggs
1 tablespoon cooking oil

2 teaspoons stevia blend
  or ¼ tsp. stevioside
  or 4 packets of stevia
¼ teaspoon salt

In a medium mixing bowl, combine flour and stevia; mix well. Add milk, eggs, oil, and salt. Beat till mixed well. Lightly grease a 6-inch skillet; heat. Remove from heat. Spoon 2 tablespoons of the batter into hot pan. Lift and tilt the skillet to spread batter into a thin circle. Return to heat. Brown on one side only. Remove crepe; place on paper towels. Repeat with remaining batter; greasing skillet as needed.

Makes 18 crepes.

NUTRITIONAL DATA (PER SERVING): 52 CALORIES; 2G TOTAL FAT; 2G PROTEIN; 6G CARBOHYDRATE • FOOD EXCHANGES: ½ STARCH; ½ FAT

Cream Puffs

1/2 cup butter
1 cup water
1/8 teaspoon salt
1 cup all-purpose flour
1 teaspoon stevia blend
  or 1/8 tsp. stevioside
  or 2 packets of stevia

4 each eggs
Powdered Sugar Replacement,
  optional (see index)

Filling:
pudding, whipped cream, ice
  cream, or fresh fruit

In a small bowl, combine flour and stevia, mix well, and set aside. In a heavy saucepan, combine butter, 1 cup water, and salt. Bring to a boil. While stirring vigorously, add flour mixture to boiling water all at once. Cook, stirring constantly, till mixture forms a ball. Remove from heat; cool slightly. Beating with a wooden spoon, add eggs one at a time. Beat till dough is smooth.

On a greased baking sheet, drop heaping tablespoons of batter 3 inches apart. Bake in a 400°F oven for 30 to 35 minutes or till golden. Cool. Cut puffs in half, and remove any excess dough from inside. Fill with your favorite filling. Sift Powdered Sugar Replacement over tops, if desired.

Makes 10.

NUTRITIONAL DATA (PER SERVING): 232 CALORIES; 11G TOTAL FAT; 4G PROTEIN; 29G CARBOHYDRATE • FOOD EXCHANGES: 1/2 STARCH; 1/2 LEAN MEAT; 2 FAT; 1 1/2 OTHER CARBOHYDRATES

Peanut Butter Balls

8 tablespoons cornstarch

8 tablespoons sugar-free peanut
butter

4 teaspoons stevia blend
or ½ tsp. stevioside
or 8 packets of stevia

2 tablespoons Chocolate Chips
(see index)

Dipping Chocolate (see index) or
Powdered Sugar Replacement (see
index)

In a bowl, combine corn starch and stevia. Mix till well blended. Add peanut butter. Knead till well blended and firm. Knead in Chocolate Chips. Form into 16 round balls (about 1 tablespoon each). Dip in Dipping Chocolate, or coat with Powdered Sugar Replacement. Serve immediately or store in refrigerator.

Makes 16 servings.

NUTRITIONAL DATA (PER SERVING): 67 CALORIES; 4G TOTAL FAT; 2G PROTEIN; 6G CARBOHY-DRATE • FOOD EXCHANGES: ½ STARCH

Fudge Balls

¹/₃ cup butter
3 tablespoons cream
1 teaspoon vanilla extract
¹/₄ cup Dutch cocoa powder

1 cup Powdered Sugar
   Replacement (see index)
Dipping Chocolate (see index) *or*
   flaked coconut

In a bowl, beat butter, cream, and vanilla till creamy. Mix in cocoa powder and Powdered Sugar Replacement. Knead until dough is smooth. Form into small balls. Dip balls in Dipping Chocolate, cool completely, dip again, and cool.

Makes 40 balls.

NUTRITIONAL DATA (PER SERVING): 18 CALORIES; 2G TOTAL FAT; TRACE PROTEIN; TRACE CARBOHYDRATE • FOOD EXCHANGES: ¹/₂ FAT

Variation:

Prepare as above, but instead of dipping, roll in flaked coconut, or chopped nuts.

Chocolate Fudge Treats

1 ounce unsweetened chocolate,
  cut up
8 teaspoons stevia blend
  or 1 tsp. stevioside
  or 16 packets of stevia

1 teaspoon vanilla
1 cup instant powdered milk
$1/3$ cup cream
$1/4$ cup butter

Over a double boiler, melt unsweetened chocolate and butter at medium heat stirring constantly. Do not let water boil. Still stirring constantly, add 8 teaspoons stevia blend and cream, continuing to cook till heated thoroughly. Remove from heat. Using an electric mixer on medium-low, slowly add the powdered milk. Continue adding powdered milk till a soft dough forms. Shape dough into small bite-sized squares. Serve immediately or cool in the refrigerator. Makes about 1 dozen.

NUTRITIONAL DATA (PER SERVING): 123 CALORIES; 10G TOTAL FAT; 3G PROTEIN; 5G CARBOHYDRATE • FOOD EXCHANGES: 2 FAT

Chocolate Chips

1 cup nonfat dry milk powder

2 ounces unsweetened bakers
   chocolate, chopped

3 tablespoons paraffin wax

$^1/_2$ cup milk

1 tablespoon stevia blend
   or $^3/_8$ tsp. stevioside
   or 6 packets of stevia

In a food processor or blender, combine powdered milk, stevia, chopped chocolate, and paraffin; blend to a powder. In a double boiler, combine milk and chocolate mixture. Stirring constantly, cook until chocolate and paraffin are melted. Mixture should be thick and smooth. Remove from heat. Allow to cool slightly. Spread chocolate mixture on wax paper. Allow chocolate to set overnight. Remove chocolate from wax paper, and break into small pieces. If chocolate does not remove easily, warm the back of the waxed paper with your hands. Store in the refrigerator.

NUTRITIONAL DATA (PER SERVING): 1006 CALORIES; 70G TOTAL FAT; 44G PROTEIN; 71G CARBOHYDRATE • FOOD EXCHANGES: 1 STARCH; $^1/_2$ LEAN MEAT; 14 FAT

Variation:

Dipping Chocolate: Follow directions above, but when mixture is done, do not cool. Keep chocolate slightly warm. Dip candies using a dipping spoon. Shake off excess chocolate. Place on waxed paper and allow to cool completely. Store in the refrigerator.

Powdered Sugar Replacement

2 cups powdered milk

2 cups cornstarch

16 tablespoons stevia blend

or 8 tsp. stevioside

or 96 packets of stevia

In a food processor or blender, mix all ingredients to a fine powder. Store in airtight container.

Makes about 5 cups.

Use this versatile recipe to make Fudge Balls (see Index) or sprinkle over buttered toast. For a decorative touch, lightly sift over frosted cakes or cookies. Powdered Sugar Replacement is *not* intended to replace powdered sugar in conventional sugar sweetened recipes.

NUTRITIONAL DATA (PER SERVING): 449 CALORIES; 14G TOTAL FAT; 14G PROTEIN; 66G CARBOHYDRATE • FOOD EXCHANGES: 3 STARCH; 3 FAT

CHAPTER 13

Tempting Toppings, Dessert Sauces & Fruit Preserves

TEMPTING TOPPINGS, DESSERT SAUCES & FRUIT PRESERVES

Apple Butter – 233

Apricot Rum Sauce – 222

Banana Sauce – 223

Bittersweet Chocolate Glaze – 216

Blueberry Syrup – 227

Butterscotch Sauce – 221

Chantilly Cream Frosting – 214

Cherry Sauce – 224

Chocolate Cream Cheese Frosting – 217

Chocolate Sauce – 218

Chocolate Whipped Cream – 232

Cinnamon Stevia – 230

Freezer Jam – 235

Fruit Juice Jelly – 236

Hot Fudge Sauce – 219

Lite Whipped Topping – 231

Low-Fat Strawberry Cream Cheese Spread – 229

Maple Flavored Syrup – 228

Mocha Sauce – 220

Orange or Lemon Cream Cheese Glaze – 215

Orange Sauce – 225

Peach Butter – 234

Stevia Butter – 230

Stirred Custard Sauce – 226

Vanilla Cream Cheese Frosting – 213

Whipped Cream – 232

Vanilla Cream Cheese Frosting

EXCELLENT FOR CAKES, MUFFINS, AND COOKIES.

2 8-oz. packages cream cheese
4 teaspoons stevia blend
  or ¹/₂ tsp. stevioside

or 8 packets of stevia
1 teaspoon vanilla

In a mixing bowl, beat cream cheese at medium speed till fluffy. Sprinkle stevia blend over cream cheese. Beat well, using a rubber spatula to scrape the sides of the bowl often. Add vanilla; beat till combined. Frosts 1 cake. Refrigerate unused portions up to 5 days.

Makes about 2 cups.

NUTRITIONAL DATA (PER SERVING): 798 CALORIES; 79G TOTAL FAT; 17G PROTEIN; 7G CARBOHYDRATE • FOOD EXCHANGES: 2¹/₂ LEAN MEAT; 14¹/₂ FAT

Chantilly Cream Frosting

4 tablespoons cornstarch
1 cup skim milk
4 teaspoons stevia blend
  or $^1/_2$ tsp. stevioside

  or 8 packets of stevia
5 tablespoons powdered milk
2 teaspoons vanilla
$^3/_4$ cup butter

Mix cornstarch, skim milk, stevia, and powdered milk in a saucepan. Cook until thickened, stirring constantly. Remove from heat, and add vanilla. Allow to cool completely. In a bowl, whip butter till creamy. Add the cooled mixture to butter and beat well. Refrigerate until ready to use.

Makes about 2 cups – enough to ice a two layer cake.

NUTRITIONAL DATA (PER SERVING): 825 CALORIES; 75G TOTAL FAT; 10G PROTEIN; 30G CARBOHYDRATE • FOOD EXCHANGES: 1 STARCH; 15 FAT

Orange or Lemon
Cream Cheese Glaze

1 8-oz. package reduced-fat
  cream cheese, softened
1 teaspoon orange or lemon extract
$1\frac{1}{2}$ teaspoons stevia blend

or $^3/_{16}$ tsp. stevioside
or 3 packets of stevia
skim milk

Mix cream cheese, extract, stevia blend, and enough milk to make medium glaze consistency.

Makes about 1 cup.

Perfect over angel food cake or lemon cake. Makes a nice glaze for cookies.

NUTRITIONAL DATA (PER SERVING): 549 CALORIES; 40G TOTAL FAT; 26G PROTEIN; 19G CARBOHYDRATE • FOOD EXCHANGES: $3\frac{1}{2}$ LEAN MEAT; 6 FAT; $\frac{1}{2}$ OTHER CARBOHYDRATES

Bittersweet Chocolate Glaze

TRY DRIZZLING OVER CAKE OR ICE CREAM.
MAKES A GREAT FONDUE.

3 ounces unsweetened baking
   chocolate, cut into small pieces
1/4 cup skim milk
1 tablespoon butter

5 teaspoons stevia blend
   or 5/8 tsp. stevioside
   or 10 packets of stevia

Combine chocolate, stevia blend, and milk in small saucepan or double boiler. Cook over low heat, stirring frequently, just until chocolate begins to melt. Remove from heat. Stir until mixture is smooth. Allow to cool until glaze is thick enough to spread.

Makes about 1/2 cup.

NUTRITIONAL DATA (PER SERVING): 567 CALORIES; 59G TOTAL FAT; 11G PROTEIN; 27G CARBOHYDRATE • FOOD EXCHANGES: 1 1/2 STARCH; 1/2 LEAN MEAT; 11 1/2 FAT

Chocolate Cream Cheese Frosting

THIS DECADENT TOPPING IS OUR FAMILY'S FAVORITE.

2 8-oz. packages fat-free cream
  cheese, at room temperature
7 teaspoons stevia blend
  or ⁷/₈ tsp. stevioside

or 14 packets of stevia
3 tablespoons skim milk
¹/₃ cup Dutch-process cocoa
1 teaspoon vanilla

In a medium mixing bowl, beat cream cheese, stevia, and 1 tablespoon milk until fluffy. Beat in cocoa, vanilla, and enough remaining milk to bring frosting to a spreadable consistency.

Makes about 2 cups.

NUTRITIONAL DATA (PER SERVING): 578 CALORIES; 43G TOTAL FAT; 27G PROTEIN; 23G CARBOHYDRATE • FOOD EXCHANGES: ¹/₂ STARCH; 4 LEAN MEAT; 6 FAT; ¹/₂ OTHER CARBOHY-DRATES

Chocolate Sauce

SERVE HOT OVER ICE CREAM, CAKE, WAFFLES, OR PANCAKES.

2 squares unsweetened baking chocolate

6 teaspoons stevia blend
or ³/₄ tsp. stevioside

or 12 packets of stevia

³/₄ cup skim milk

1 teaspoon vanilla

In a heavy pan or double boiler, dissolve 2 tablespoons stevia blend with ³/₄ cup of skim milk. Add the baking chocolate; heat, stirring, until chocolate is melted. Remove from heat and stir in vanilla.

Makes about 1 cup.

NUTRITIONAL DATA (PER SERVING): 373 CALORIES; 32G TOTAL FAT; 12G PROTEIN; 26G CARBOHYDRATE • FOOD EXCHANGES: 1 STARCH; ¹/₂ LEAN MEAT; 6 FAT

Hot Fudge Sauce

A SUGAR-FREE VERSION OF THE REAL THING.

1 ounce unsweetened chocolate,
  cut up
8 teaspoons stevia blend
  or 1 tsp. stevioside
  or 16 packets of stevia

1 teaspoon vanilla
$^1/_2$ cup powdered milk
$^1/_2$ cup whipping cream.
$^1/_4$ cup butter

Over a double boiler, melt unsweetened chocolate and butter at medium heat, stirring frequently. Do not let water boil. Stir in 8 teaspoons stevia blend and cream; allow to simmer, stirring occasionally, until heated thoroughly. Remove from heat. Using an electric mixer on medium-low, slowly add powdered milk. Serve over ice cream or cake. Refrigerate any unused portion for up to 5 days.

NUTRITIONAL DATA (PER SERVING): 1295 CALORIES; 123G TOTAL FAT; 23G PROTEIN; 37G CARBOHYDRATE • FOOD EXCHANGES: $^1/_2$ STARCH; 24$^1/_2$ FAT

Mocha Sauce

1 cup skim milk
4 teaspoons unsweetened cocoa
2 teaspoons cornstarch
1 teaspoon instant coffee crystals

1 teaspoon vanilla
2 teaspoons stevia blend *or*
  $^1/_4$ tsp. stevioside
  or 4 packets of stevia

In small, heavy saucepan, combine milk, cocoa, cornstarch, stevia, and coffee crystals. Cook, stirring constantly, until thickened and boiling. Reduce heat; continue cooking and stirring 2 more minutes. Remove from heat, stir in vanilla, and cool. Cover and refrigerate till cold.

Makes about 1 cup.

NUTRITIONAL DATA (PER SERVING): 172 CALORIES; 3G TOTAL FAT; 13G PROTEIN; 30G CARBOHYDRATE • FOOD EXCHANGES: 1 STARCH; $^1/_2$ LEAN MEAT; 0 FRUIT; $^1/_2$ FAT

Butterscotch Sauce

SERVE OVER VANILLA ICE CREAM, CREPES, OR FLAN.

1 cup apple juice
1 tablespoon cornstarch
1 tablespoon margarine
4 teaspoons stevia blend

or $^1/_2$ tsp. stevioside
or 8 packets of stevia
1 teaspoon butterscotch flavoring
1 teaspoon vanilla

Combine apple juice, stevia, and cornstarch in small saucepan. Cook, stirring constantly, over medium heat until thick and bubbly. Continue cooking and stirring 2 more minutes. Remove from heat. Stir in margarine, butterscotch flavoring, and vanilla.

Makes 1 cup.

NUTRITIONAL DATA (PER SERVING): 261 CALORIES; 12G TOTAL FAT; TRACE PROTEIN; 38G CARBOHYDRATE • FOOD EXCHANGES: $^1/_2$ STARCH; 1 $^1/_2$ FRUIT; 2 $^1/_2$ FAT

Apricot Rum Sauce

EXCELLENT FOR WAFFLES, PANCAKES, OR ICE CREAM.

4 each ripe apricots, pealed and
  pitted
2 tablespoons rum flavoring
$^1/_2$ cup water

1 each lemon juice
1 $^1/_2$ teaspoons stevia blend
  or $^3/_{16}$ tsp. stevioside
  or 3 packets of stevia

Combine apricots, water, stevia, and lemon juice in a heavy sauce pan and heat over medium heat stirring frequently until apricots soften; bring to a boil. Remove from heat and add the rum flavoring; allow to cool. In a blender or food processor, puree sauce till thick and creamy. Refrigerate; serve cold.

NUTRITIONAL DATA (PER SERVING): 111 CALORIES; 1G TOTAL FAT; 3G PROTEIN; 22G CARBO-HYDRATE • FOOD EXCHANGES: 1 $^1/_2$ FRUIT

Variations:

Plums or peaches can be substituted for the apricots.

Note: The fruit must be very ripe or the sauce will be tart.

Banana Sauce

1 each banana, thinly sliced
1/2 each lemon, or 1 tablespoon
   lemon juice
1 tablespoon maraschino liqueur
1 1/2 teaspoons stevia blend

or 3/16 tsp. stevioside
or 3 packets of stevia
2 teaspoons arrowroot or
   cornstarch

Put the lemon juice, water, and maraschino liqueur into a pan with stevia, and dissolve stevia over low heat, stirring frequently. Make a paste of the arrowroot or cornstarch with a tablespoon of water. Stir paste into the hot liquid and cook, stirring constantly, until the sauce thickens and is clear. Add the sliced banana and serve hot.

Makes a perfect filling for crepes, or a topping for pancakes, waffles, or ice cream.

NUTRITIONAL DATA (PER SERVING): 133 CALORIES; 1G TOTAL FAT; 1G PROTEIN; 34G CARBO-HYDRATE • FOOD EXCHANGES: 1/2 STARCH; 2 FRUIT

Cherry Sauce

1 pound cherries, pitted
1 1/2 teaspoons stevia blend
  or 3/16 tsp. stevioside
  or 3 packets of stevia
1 pinch ground cinnamon

1/2 cup water
1 teaspoon lemon juice
2 teaspoons arrowroot
1 tablespoon water

Combine pitted cherries and lemon juice in a pan with stevia blend. Cover and set on low heat until the juice runs freely. Remove cherries with a slotted spoon leaving the juice in the pan. Set cherries aside. Add 1/2 cup water to the juice; simmer 5 minutes uncovered, stirring occasionally. Taste for sweetness and adjust to your liking. If too sweet, add a little more lemon juice. Make a paste of the arrowroot with 1 tablespoon of water. Stir paste into the cherry syrup. Bring, stirring, just to a boil; remove from heat. The liquid should be the consistency of heavy cream. Add the cherries to the pan; stir till well mixed.

Makes about 3 cups.

Cherry sauce is excellent over cakes, over ice cream, or as a filling for crepes.

NUTRITIONAL DATA (PER SERVING): 77 CALORIES; 1G TOTAL FAT; 1G PROTEIN; 18G CARBOHY-DRATE • FOOD EXCHANGES: 1 1/2 FRUIT

Orange Sauce

¾ cup orange juice
1 tablespoon cornstarch
1 ½ teaspoons stevia blend

or ³/₁₆ tsp. stevioside
or 3 packets of stevia

In a small, heavy saucepan, mix orange juice, stevia, and cornstarch; heat to boiling stirring constantly. Reduce heat. Simmer, stirring constantly, until thickened (about 3 minutes). Remove from heat. Cool to room temperature; refrigerate until chilled.

Makes 6 2-tablespoon servings.

NUTRITIONAL DATA (PER SERVING): 19 CALORIES; 0 TOTAL FAT; 0 PROTEIN; 4G CARBOHY-DRATE • FOOD EXCHANGES: FREE

Stirred Custard Sauce

3 each eggs, beaten
2 cups light cream
3 teaspoons stevia blend

or ³/₈ tsp. stevioside
or 6 packets of stevia
1 teaspoon vanilla

In a heavy, medium saucepan, combine eggs, cream, and stevia. Cook, stirring constantly, over medium heat until the custard just coats a metal spoon. Remove from heat and stir in vanilla. Pour custard mixture into a bowl. Cover surface with clear plastic wrap. Chill till serving time. Create your own flavor by adding 3 tablespoons of flavored liqueur instead of the vanilla.

Makes 6-8 servings.

The perfect addition to bread pudding, cake, or to top off fruit. Also makes a delicious fondue for cubes of cake or sliced fruit.

NUTRITIONAL DATA (PER SERVING): 143 CALORIES; 13G TOTAL FAT; 4G PROTEIN; 3G CARBO-HYDRATE • FOOD EXCHANGES: ¹/₂ LEAN MEAT; 2¹/₂ FAT

Blueberry Syrup

1 cup blueberries
1/2 cup apple juice
1 1/2 teaspoons cornstarch
2 teaspoons stevia blend

or 1/4 tsp. stevioside
or 4 packets of stevia
1 tablespoon lemon juice
1 tablespoon margarine or butter

Combine berries and apple juice in a blender or food processor; blend till pureed. In a heavy saucepan, combine blueberry puree, stevia, and cornstarch; mix well. Cook, stirring constantly, till thick and bubbly. Continue cooking and stirring for 2 more minutes. Remove from heat. Stir in lemon juice and butter.

Makes 1 cup.

Serve over pancakes, waffles, or French toast.

NUTRITIONAL DATA (PER SERVING): 260 CALORIES; 12G TOTAL FAT; 1G PROTEIN; 40G CARBOHYDRATE • FOOD EXCHANGES: 2 1/2 FRUIT; 2 1/2 FAT

Maple Flavored Syrup

1 cup apple juice
1 tablespoon cornstarch
1 tablespoon margarine
3 teaspoons stevia blend

or ³/₈ tsp. stevioside
or 6 packets of stevia
1 teaspoon maple flavoring
1 teaspoon vanilla

Combine apple juice, stevia and cornstarch in small saucepan. Stirring constantly, cook, over medium heat until thick and bubbly. Continue cooking and stirring 2 minutes more. Remove from heat. Stir in margarine, maple flavoring, and vanilla.

Makes 1 cup.

Serve over pancakes, waffles, or French toast.

NUTRITIONAL DATA (PER SERVING): 261 CALORIES; 12G TOTAL FAT; TRACE PROTEIN; 38G CARBOHYDRATE • FOOD EXCHANGES: ¹/₂ STARCH; 1 ¹/₂ FRUIT; 2¹/₂ FAT

Low-Fat Strawberry Cream Cheese Spread

GREAT ON TOAST OR BAGELS.

1 8-ounces package low-fat cream
  cheese, at room temperature
2 teaspoons stevia blend

or ¹/₈ tsp. stevioside
or 4 packets of stevia
¹/₂ teaspoon strawberry flavoring

In a mixing bowl, beat cream cheese at medium speed till fluffy. Sprinkle stevia blend over cream cheese. Beat well, scraping sides of bowl often. Add strawberry flavoring. Beat till thoroughly combined. Serve immediately. Refrigerate any unused portions for up to 5 days.

Makes about 1 cup.

NUTRITIONAL DATA (PER SERVING): 524 CALORIES; 40G TOTAL FAT; 24G PROTEIN; 16G CARBOHYDRATE • FOOD EXCHANGES: 3¹/₂ LEAN MEAT;0 FRUIT; 6 FAT; ¹/₂ OTHER CARBOHY-DRATES

Stevia Butter

¹/₂ cup butter, room temperature	*or* ¹/₈ tsp. stevioside
1 teaspoon stevia blend	*or* 2 packets of stevia

In a small mixing bowl, cream butter till fluffy. Sprinkle stevia blend over the butter. Mix well, scraping the sides of the bowl often. Serve immediately. Refrigerate any unused portions.

Makes about ¹/₂ cup (four 2-tablespoon servings).

NUTRITIONAL DATA (PER SERVING): 203 CALORIES; 23G TOTAL FAT; TRACE PROTEIN; TRACE CARBOHYDRATE • FOOD EXCHANGES: 4¹/₂ FAT

Cinnamon Stevia

¹/₂ cup powdered milk	*or* ¹/₄ tsp. stevioside
1 tablespoon cinnamon	*or* 4 packets of stevia
2 teaspoons stevia blend	

Combine all ingredients in a blender or food processor. Process until it has the consistency of flour. Sift over cake, cookies, pancakes, waffles, or French toast.

Makes nine 1-tablespoon servings.

NUTRITIONAL DATA (PER SERVING): 37 CALORIES; 2G TOTAL FAT; 2G PROTEIN; 3G CARBOHYDRATE • FOOD EXCHANGES: ¹/₂ FAT

Lite Whipped Topping

12 ounces evaporated milk
1/3 cup water
1 package gelatin

2 teaspoons stevia blend
   or 1/4 tsp. stevioside
   or 4 packets of stevia
1 teaspoon vanilla

Refrigerate can of condensed milk till well chilled, at least 4 hours. In a small saucepan, mix cold water and gelatin; allow to sit for five minutes. Over medium heat, cook gelatin mixture till bubbly. Allow to cool to room temperature. Make an ice bath: take a large bowl and fill with ice, placing a smaller bowl on top of the ice. Pour the condensed milk, gelatin mixture, stevia, and vanilla in smaller bowl.

On high speed of an electric mixer, beat milk mixture till soft peaks form. Best when served immediately. Refrigerate any unused portions for up to 5 days.

Makes about 4 cups (sixteen 1/4-cup servings).

NUTRITIONAL DATA (PER SERVING): 31 CALORIES; 2G TOTAL FAT; 2G PROTEIN; 2G CARBOHYDRATE • FOOD EXCHANGES: 1/2 FAT;

Whipped Cream

1 cup whipping cream
1 teaspoon stevia blend
  or ¹/₈ tsp. stevioside

or 2 packets of stevia
1 teaspoon vanilla

In a bowl combine whipping cream, stevia blend, and vanilla. Beat on medium speed till soft peaks form.

Makes eight ¹/₂-cup servings.

If you overbeat cream, it will turn to butter. But don't worry – just poor off the buttermilk and enjoy a sweet spread on your toast or muffin.

NUTRITIONAL DATA (PER SERVING): 104 CALORIES; 11G TOTAL FAT; 1G PROTEIN; 1G CARBO-HYDRATE • FOOD EXCHANGES: 2 FAT

Variation:

Chocolate Whipped Cream: Prepare as above, sifting in 2 tablespoons unsweetened cocoa powder plus 1 teaspoon additional stevia blend.

Apple Butter

6 cups sweet apples, peeled and
  sliced
1 cup fresh apple cider
3 teaspoons stevia blend

or $^3/_8$ tsp. stevioside
or 6 packets of stevia
1 teaspoon ground cinnamon
  (optional)

In a heavy saucepan, place apples and cider over medium heat.
Stirring frequently, cook until mixture comes to a boil. Lower heat and
simmer, still stirring frequently, for about 60 minutes, or till apples
have disintegrated and mixture is thick. Remove from heat. Stir in
stevia and cinnamon, if desired. Pour into jars and refrigerate for up to
2 weeks.

Makes sixteen 2-tablespoon servings.

Use as a spread or as a dessert topping.

NUTRITIONAL DATA (PER SERVING): 32 CALORIES; TRACE TOTAL FAT; TRACE PROTEIN; 8G
CARBOHYDRATE • FOOD EXCHANGES: $^1/_2$ FRUIT

Peach Butter

3 pounds peaches, peeled, pitted
   and sliced
3/4 cup white grape juice
1–2 teaspoons ground cinnamon
$^1/_2$ teaspoon ground nutmeg

$^1/_8$ teaspoon ground cloves
8 teaspoons stevia blend
   or 1 tsp. stevioside
   or 16 packets of stevia

In a large, heavy saucepan, combine peaches, juice, spices, and stevia. Stirring occasionally, bring to boiling. Cover and simmer until fruit can be easily mashed with a fork (about 15 minutes). Cool slightly. Puree in blender or food processor. Return to saucepan. Simmer, uncovered, over low heat until desired consistency, stirring frequently. (This may take up to 1 hour.) Remove from heat. Transfer to freezer containers or jars, leaving a $^1/_2$-inch head space. Place in the refrigerator until cool (about 3 hours). Transfer to the freezer. Store up to 2 weeks in refrigerator or up to 3 months in freezer.

Makes 6 cups (twenty-four 2-tablespoon servings).

NUTRITIONAL DATA (PER SERVING): 24 CALORIES; TRACE TOTAL FAT; TRACE PROTEIN; 6G CARBOHYDRATE • FOOD EXCHANGES: $^1/_2$ FRUIT

Freezer Jam

3 cups crushed fruit, room
  temperature
1 package fruit pectin for sugar-
  free jams and jellies
5–7 teaspoons stevia blend

or $5/8$–1 tsp. stevioside
or 10–14 packets of stevia
  (depending on sweetness of
  fruit)
1 cup water

In a bowl, combine the crushed fruit with stevia; set aside. Pour 1 cup of water in a heavy saucepan. Stir the pectin into the water slowly to prevent lumping. Stirring constantly, bring pectin-water mixture to a boil. Boil 2 minutes more, still stirring constantly. Pour the hot pectin-water mixture into crushed fruit. Stir thoroughly, about 4 minutes. Pour into freezer containers, leaving a $1/2$-inch head space; cover with tight-fitting lids, and refrigerate. After jam has set (about 3 hours), transfer to freezer. Makes an excellent cake filling, or ice-cream topping.

Makes 2 cups (thirty-two 2-tablespoon servings).

NUTRITIONAL DATA (PER SERVING): 6 CALORIES; TRACE TOTAL FAT; TRACE PROTEIN; 2G CARBOHYDRATE • FOOD EXCHANGES: 0 EXCHANGES

Fruit Juice Jelly

FAST AND EASY; FOR THE FREEZER OR THE REFRIGERATOR.

1 pkg. fruit pectin for sugar-free
  jams and jellies
4 cups your favorite juice

7–10 teaspoons stevia blend
  or $^7/_8$–$1^1/_4$ tsp. stevioside
  or 14–20 packets of stevia

In a heavy saucepan, combine juice and one package of lite fruit pectin. Let mixture set 5–10 minutes, then bring to a full boil over high heat, stirring constantly. Boil for 2 minutes longer, still stirring constantly. Remove from heat and add stevia to taste. Stir well. Pour into clean freezer containers, leaving a $^1/_2$-inch head space; cover with tight-fitting lid, and refrigerate. After jam has set (about 3 hours), transfer to freezer.

Makes 4 cups (thirty-two 2-tablespoon servings).

NUTRITIONAL DATA (PER SERVING): 6 CALORIES; TRACE TOTAL FAT; TRACE PROTEIN; 2G CARBOHYDRATE • FOOD EXCHANGES: 0 EXCHANGES

CHAPTER 14

Condiments, Sauces & Relishes

CONDIMENTS, SAUCES & RELISHES

Old Fashioned Catsup

2 cups tomato sauce
$^1/_4$ cup apple cider vinegar
1 teaspoon stevia blend
   or $^1/_8$ tsp. stevioside
   or 2 packets of stevia

$^1/_4$ teaspoon onion powder
1 tablespoon cornstarch or
   arrowroot
1 teaspoon water

In a small cup, mix water and cornstarch or arrowroot. Stir until dissolved. In a large saucepan, combine all ingredients; mix well. Stirring constantly, bring to a gentle boil. Still stirring constantly, reduce heat and simmer to desired thickness. Refrigerate until needed.

Makes about 1$^1/_2$ cups (twelve 2-tablespoon servings).

NUTRITIONAL DATA (PER SERVING): 16 CALORIES; TRACE TOTAL FAT; 1G PROTEIN; 4G CARBOHYDRATE • FOOD EXCHANGES: $^1/_2$ VEGETABLE

Tangy Catsup

1 cup apple cider vinegar
1 teaspoon ground cinnamon
1 teaspoon celery seed
2 24-ounce cans tomatoes, diced
1/2 cup onions, minced
1/2 teaspoon red pepper

1 tablespoon salt
5 teaspoons stevia blend
  or 5/8 tsp. stevioside
  or 10 packets of stevia
2 tablespoons tomato paste

In a small saucepan, stir together vinegar, cinnamon, and celery seed; bring to a boil. Set aside. In a heavy stock pot or large saucepan, mix together remaining ingredients; bring to a boil stirring occasionally. Reduce heat. Add vinegar mix. Simmer for 30 minutes stirring occasionally. In small batches, puree in blender or food processor. Return to pot; simmer, stirring occasionally, until thick.

Makes about 4 cups (thrity-two 2-tablespoon servings).

You can speed up the thickening process by adding a paste of 2 tablespoons of cornstarch or arrowroot mixed with 1/4 cup cold water.

NUTRITIONAL DATA (PER SERVING): 11 CALORIES; TRACE TOTAL FAT; TRACE PROTEIN; 3G CARBOHYDRATE • FOOD EXCHANGES: 1/2 VEGETABLE

Variation:

Spicy Catsup: Add 3 teaspoons of hot sauce during the simmering stage.

Mexicali Barbecue Sauce

¹/₂ cup Picante Sauce (see index)
1 tablespoon tomato paste
2 teaspoons stevia blend

or ¹/₄ tsp. stevioside
or 4 packets of stevia
1 tablespoon Dijon mustard

In a bowl, dissolve stevia into picante sauce. Mix remaining ingredients into picante sauce. Stir until well mixed. Keep refrigerated until needed. Use as a baste or sauce.

Makes about 1 cup (eight 2-tablespoon servings).

NUTRITIONAL DATA (PER SERVING): 8 CALORIES; TRACE TOTAL FAT; TRACE PROTEIN; 1G CARBOHYDRATE • FOOD EXCHANGES: FREE

Mustard Barbecue Sauce

1 cup prepared yellow mustard
²/₃ cup apple cider vinegar
1 tablespoon Worcestershire
    sauce
1¹/₂ cups catsup (see index)
¹/₂ teaspoon maple flavoring

2 tablespoons olive oil
¹/₂ teaspoon black pepper
9 teaspoons stevia blend
    or 1 tsp. stevioside
    or 18 packets of stevia

Combine all ingredients in a medium sauce pan. Simmer over medium heat, stirring occasionally, until sauce is well blended and hot. Remove from heat; allow to cool. Keep refrigerated until needed. Use as a baste or sauce.

Makes about 2 cups (sixteen 2-tablespoon servings)

NUTRITIONAL DATA (PER SERVING): 52 CALORIES; 2G TOTAL FAT; 1G PROTEIN; 8G CARBOHY-DRATE • FOOD EXCHANGES: 0 FRUIT; ¹/₂ FAT; ¹/₂ OTHER CARBOHYDRATES

Cocktail Sauce

1 cup Old Fashioned Catsup (see index)

3 tablespoons grated onion

3 tablespoons prepared horse radish

2 tablespoons lemon juice

2 tablespoons minced fresh tarragon

Tabasco to taste

Wisk all ingredients in a medium bowl to blend. Cover and refrigerate at least 1 hour. For a bit more spice try using Tangy Catsup (see index).

Makes 1 1/2 cups (twelve 2-tablespoon servings).

NUTRITIONAL DATA (PER SERVING): 24 CALORIES; TRACE TOTAL FAT; TRACE PROTEIN; 6G CARBOHYDRATE • FOOD EXCHANGES: 1/2 OTHER CARBOHYDRATES

Picante Sauce

1 24-ounce can tomatoes, finely diced, reserve juice
6 ounces reserved tomato juice
1 small onion, finely chopped
1 4-ounce can green chili peppers, finely chopped
2 tablespoons fresh cilantro, minced
1 tablespoon lime juice
2 teaspoons stevia blend
   or ¹/₄ tsp. stevioside
   or 4 packets of stevia
1 teaspoon salt
1 teaspoon pepper
1 each jalapeno, finely chopped

In a bowl, combine all ingredients; mix well. Refrigerate at least 2 hours.

Makes about 4 cups (thrity-two 2-tablespoon servings).

Note: If you like it HOT, add an extra jalapeno or two, or, for the really brave, add a finely chopped Habanero pepper.

NUTRITIONAL DATA (PER SERVING): 8 CALORIES; TRACE TOTAL FAT; TRACE PROTEIN; 2G CARBOHYDRATE • FOOD EXCHANGES: ¹/₂ VEGETABLE

Black Bean Salsa

3 medium tomatoes, finely diced
1 15-ounces can black beans, drained
1 4-ounce can green chili peppers, drained, finely chopped
3 tablespoons cilantro, fresh, chopped
1 small onion, finely chopped
1 clove garlic, minced
1 each jalapeno, finely chopped
1 teaspoon stevia blend
   or $^1/_8$ tsp. stevioside
   or 2 packets of stevia
3 tablespoons lime juice
$^1/_4$ teaspoon cinnamon
salt and pepper to taste

In a small bowl, dissolve stevia into the lime juice. Set aside. In another bowl combine all of the other ingredients. Add lime mixture; mix well. Refrigerate at least 2 hours before serving.

Makes about 4$^1/_2$ cups (thirty-six 2-tablespoon servings).

Note: If you like it HOT, add an extra jalapeno or two, or, for the really brave, add a finely chopped Habanero pepper.

NUTRITIONAL DATA (PER SERVING): 15 CALORIES; TRACE TOTAL FAT; 1G PROTEIN; 3G CARBOHYDRATE • FOOD EXCHANGES: 0 EXCHANGES

Corn Relish

2 15-ounce cans corn, drained
$^1/_2$ cup celery, chopped
$^3/_4$ cup sweet red bell pepper, diced
$^3/_4$ cup green bell pepper, diced
1 medium onion, chopped
1 $^1/_4$ cups apple cider vinegar
9 teaspoons stevia blend

or 1 tsp. stevioside
or 18 packets of stevia
1 tablespoon salt
1 teaspoon celery seed
$^1/_4$ cup flour
1 tablespoon dry mustard
$^1/_2$ teaspoon ground turmeric

In a kettle, combine corn, celery, red and green peppers, onion, $^3/_4$ cup vinegar, stevia, salt, and celery seed. Bring to a boil stirring occasionally. In a small bowl combine $^1/_2$ cup vinegar, flour, dry mustard, and turmeric. Add to corn mixture. Stirring constantly, bring to a boil. Continue cooking and stirring 1 minute more. Ladle into pint jars. Refrigerate.

Makes 3 pints (forty-eight 2-tablespoon servings).

NUTRITIONAL DATA (PER SERVING): 18 CALORIES; TRACE TOTAL FAT; 1G PROTEIN; 4G CARBOHYDRATE • FOOD EXCHANGES: 0 EXCHANGES

Refrigerator Sweet Pickles

FAST AND EASY

4 cups cucumbers, thinly sliced

2 cloves garlic, halved

1 3/4 cups water

1 teaspoon mustard seed

1 teaspoon celery seed

1 teaspoon ground turmeric

2 cups onions, sliced

1 cup carrots, julienne-strip

2 cups apple cider vinegar

9 teaspoons stevia blend

or 1 tsp. stevioside

or 18 packets of stevia

Place sliced cucumbers and garlic in a glass bowl. (Do not use metal.) Set aside. In a saucepan, stir together turmeric, mustard seed, celery seed, stevia, and water. Bring to boiling. Stir in onions and carrots. Boil for 2 minutes. Stir in vinegar; cook 1 minute more. Pour over cucumbers and garlic. Cool. Cover and refrigerate at least 24 hours before serving.

Makes about 5 cups (twenty 1/4-cup servings).

NUTRITIONAL DATA (PER SERVING): 17 CALORIES; TRACE TOTAL FAT; TRACE PROTEIN; 4G CARBOHYDRATE • FOOD EXCHANGES: 1/2 VEGETABLE

Cranberry Sauce

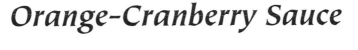

1 12-ounce package fresh
  cranberries
9 teaspoons stevia blend

or 1 tsp. stevioside
or 18 packets of stevia
1 cup white grape juice

In a saucepan, combine stevia and juice. Bring to a rapid boil. Add cranberries. Stirring constantly, boil gently over medium-high heat for 6–7 minutes or until cranberry skins pop. Remove from heat. Serve warm or chilled.

Makes about 3 cups (twelve $1/4$-cup servings).

NUTRITIONAL DATA (PER SERVING): 28 CALORIES; TRACE TOTAL FAT; TRACE PROTEIN; 7G CARBOHYDRATE • FOOD EXCHANGES: $1/2$ FRUIT

Orange-Cranberry Sauce

1 12-ounce package fresh
  cranberries
10 teaspoons stevia blend
  or 1 $1/4$ tsp. stevioside

or 20 packets of stevia
1 cup orange juice
1 teaspoon orange flavoring

In a saucepan, combine stevia and juice. Bring to a rapid boil stirring constantly. Add cranberries. Still stirring constantly, boil gently over medium-high heat for 6–7 minutes or until cranberry skins pop. Remove from heat and stir in orange flavoring. Serve warm or chilled.

Makes about 3 cups (twelve $1/4$-cup servings).

NUTRITIONAL DATA (PER SERVING): 24 CALORIES; TRACE TOTAL FAT; TRACE PROTEIN; 6G CARBOHYDRATE • FOOD EXCHANGES: $1/2$ FRUIT

Sweet & Sour Sauce

$^3/_4$ cup water
$^1/_3$ cup catsup (see index)
$^1/_3$ cup apple cider vinegar or
　white wine vinegar
1 tablespoon soy sauce

2 tablespoons cornstarch or
　arrowroot
5 teaspoons stevia blend
　or $^5/_8$ tsp. stevioside
　or 10 packets of stevia

In a heavy saucepan, combine water, vinegar, ketchup, stevia and soy sauce. Stir in cornstarch. Over medium heat, cook, stirring constantly, until thick and bubbly, then continue cooking and stirring for 1 minute more. Remove from heat. Serve over vegetables, meat or meat substitute.

Makes about 1 cup (four $^1/_4$-cup servings).

NUTRITIONAL DATA (PER SERVING): 41 CALORIES; TRACE TOTAL FAT; 1G PROTEIN; 11G CARBOHYDRATE • FOOD EXCHANGES: $^1/_2$ OTHER CARBOHYDRATES

White Sauce

1 tablespoon butter
1 tablespoon all-purpose flour
$^1/_2$ teaspoon stevia blend

or $^1/_{16}$ tsp. stevioside
or 1 packet of stevia
$^3/_4$ cup milk

In a saucepan, melt butter. Stir in flour, salt, stevia and pepper. Stirring constantly, cook till golden (about 2 minutes). Slowly stir in milk. Over medium heat, continue cooking and stirring until thick. Serve immediately.

Makes about $^3/_4$ cup (three $^1/_4$-cup servings).

NUTRITIONAL DATA (PER SERVING): 81 CALORIES; 6G TOTAL FAT; 2G PROTEIN; 5G CARBOHYDRATE • FOOD EXCHANGES: 1 FAT

Appendix

Stevia Conversions

For best results, use stevia extracts that contain at least 90% steviosides and read Chapters 4, Successful Cooking With Stevia.

Packets to Packets

Sugar	Stevia Blends (Spoonable Stevia)	Aspartame	Saccharin	Acesulfame-k	Sucralose (Splenda®)
1 packet	1 packet	1 packet	1 packet	1 packet	1 packet

Packets to packets stevia blends are equal in sweetening power to artificial sweeteners. However, stevia blends (spoonable stevia) in bulk are not necessarily equal to the spoonable or bulk forms of artificial sweeteners. Fortunately, most recipes call for packets of artificial sweeteners. Just convert the number of artificial sweetener packets to stevia blend (spoonable stevia), or if you prefer, use pure stevioside.

When replacing aspartame with stevia you must make some adjustments – stevia is heat stable, but aspartame will loose its sweetness when heated.

Artificial Sweetener Packets to Stevia Extracts

Artificial Sweetener (packets) or Sucralose (packets)	Stevia Blends (packets)	Stevia Blends (Spoonable Stevia) Bulk Form (teaspoons)	Clear Stevia Liquid (teaspoons)	Pure Stevioside (teaspoons)
1	1	$1/2$	about $1/4$	$1/16$
6	6	3	about $1/2$	$3/8$
8	8	4	about $3/4$	$1/2$
12	12	6	$1 1/4$	$3/4$
18	18	9	$1 1/3$	$1 1/8$
24	24	12	$2 1/2$	$1 1/2$
48	48	24	$5 1/4$	3

Avoid a Bitter Taste: Although stevia sweetening strengths vary form one brand to the next, when you use a brand high in steviosides, you can achieve a sweeter taste without bitterness. Therefore, when using a pure stevioside with less than 90% steviosides reduce the amount of stevioside listed in the chart above by 30% — the final product will not be as sweet, but you'll avoid a bitter taste.

Sugar, Sucralose (Splenda®) and Stevia Extracts

Sugar	Granulated Sucralose (Granulated Splenda®)	Stevia Blends (Spoonable Stevia) in Packets (packets)	Stevia Blends (Spoonable Stevia) Bulk Form (teaspoons)	Clear Stevia Liquid (teaspoons)	Pure Stevioside (teaspoons)
2 teaspoons	2 teaspoons	1	$1/2$	about $1/4$	$1/16$
$1/4$ cup	$1/4$ cup	6	3	about $1/2$	$3/8$
$1/3$ cup	$1/3$ cup	8	4	about $3/4$	$1/2$
$1/2$ cup	$1/2$ cup	12	6	$1 1/4$	$3/4$
$3/4$ cup	$3/4$ cup	18	9	$1 3/4$	1
1 cup	1 cup	24	12	$2 1/2$	$1 1/2$
2 cups	2 cups	48	24	$5 1/4$	3

Avoid a Bitter Taste: Although stevia sweetening strengths vary form one brand to the next, when you use a brand high in steviosides, you can achieve a sweeter taste without bitterness. Therefore, when using a pure stevioside with less than 90% steviosides reduce the amount of stevioside listed in the chart above by 30% — the final product will not be as sweet, but you'll avoid a bitter taste.

Suppliers of Stevia Extracts and Plants

The following is a list of most major stevia manufactures that offer a variety of stevia products. Their stevia products are available in health food stores or direct from the manufacture. This list is for informational purposes only to help you, the consumer, locate stevia supplements. Visit www.CookingWithStevia.com for updates.

NOW Foods
395 S. Glen Ellen Rd.
Bloomingdale, IL 60108
www.nowvitamins.com
800-999-8069

NuNaturals
2220 W. 2nd Ave. #1
Eugene, OR 97402
www.nunaturals.com
800-753-4372

Omega Nutrition/Body Ecology
6515 Aldrich rd
Bellingham, WA 98226
www.omegaflo.com
800-661-3529

Optimum Nutrition
600 N. Commerce St.
Aurora, IL 60504
optimumnutr.com
800-705-5226

Stevita Co., Inc.
(Certified Organic Stevia)
7650 US Hwy. 287, #100
Arlington, Texas 76001
www.stevitastevia.com
888-STEVITA
888-783-8482

Wisdom of the Ancients
640 S. Perry Lane #2
Tempe, AZ 85287
www.wisdomherbs.com
800-899-9908

If you are interested in growing your own stevia plants, here are three fine companies that sell stevia plants:

Canterbury Farms
http://www.spiritone.com/
~ canfarms/index.html
16185 SW 108th Ave.
Tigard, OR 97224
503-968-8269 or Fax: 503-968-6436

The Herbal Advantage
www.herbaladvantage.com
131 Bobwhite Rd.
Rogersville, MO 65742
800-753-9199

Mountain Valley Growers
www.mountainvalleygrowers.com
Sellers of Certified Organic Stevia Plants (Scientific Certification Systems).
38325 Pepperweed Rd.
Squaw Valley, CA 93675
559-338-2775

This list is only a few of the many companies that distribute stevia. For a more complete list, which is updated frequently, see the 'Cooking With Stevia' webpage at www.CookingWithStevia.com.

Stevia Petition!

Stevia is a sweetener that is currently being discriminated against by the FDA. Contact your Representative today and let them know that you want to use Stevia! Fight the injustice of the FDA!

Stevia is a natural sweetener used internationally by millions – except in the United States. This herb is being discriminated against by the Food and Drug Administration (FDA). You can fight this injustice of by contacting your government representatives today!

Photocopy this petition, fill it out and mail it to your Congressional Representative and your two Senate Representatives. With your help, we will win this battle.

This petition is also available on-line at www.CookingWithStevia.com.

NAME _____

ADDRESS _____

CITY, STATE, ZIP _____

COUNTRY _____

HOME PHONE _____

E-MAIL ADDRESS _____

DATE _____

REPRESENTATIVE'S NAME _____

REPRESENTATIVE'S ADDRESS _____

_____

Dear _____:

I am writing to express my outrage at the Food and Drug Administration's mishandling of the herb STEVIA in the United States. While other nations are able to use this wonderful herb as a sugar substitute, Americans are limited to using it as a "dietary supplement". Why is this? STEVIA is approved for use as a food and food ingredient in countries around the world because it is all-natural, non-toxic, non-caloric, helpful to the environment, a valuable cash crop and safe for diabetics, hence completely safe for human use, but FDA restricts its use by Americans. Effectively banned within the United States, STEVIA plants are rarely even grown by American farmers.

With the passage of the 1994 Dietary Supplement Health and Education Act (DSHEA), Congress rightly gave the power back to the people concerning whether or not to improve their health with the use of natural products previously kept out of reach. DSHEA also permitted Americans to use STEVIA but only as a dietary supplement. Despite this legal protection, the FDA has done everything within it's power to try to prevent the importation and distribution of STEVIA in the United States. Petitions to have STEVIA receive GRAS (Generally Accepted as Safe) status were denied by the FDA. FDA employs delay tactics, such as requesting unreasonable amounts of statistical data about this plant's agricultural and commercial history prior to 1958.

In 1997, the CBS news magazine 60 Minutes aired a report revealing a conflict of interest between FDA and one manufacturer of artificial sweeteners. This manufacturer had "influenced" the director of the FDA to get the approval of aspartame as a food additive during the 1980s when there were many questionable reports on its safety. Today the FDA receives more complaints about aspartame than about any other product. It is believed that the cozy relationship between FDA and the artificial sweetener industry is why STEVIA has largely been kept out of reach of the American consumer.

Is STEVIA safe? Absolutely. Research proves this—research the FDA ignores. Moreover, STEVIA has been used extensively around the world as an ingredient in foods WITHOUT A SINGLE CASE OF UNDESIRABLE

EFFECTS. This fact alone should qualify as proof that the product is safe for use as an all-natural sweetener.

Do the American people want STEVIA? Count on it. Americans are more and more averse to the use of artificial substances in their diets. The herb STEVIA is especially beneficial for people who suffer from diabetes, hypoglycemia, candida and other ailments where regular use of sugar and artificial sweeteners is ill-advised.

As my elected representative, I am requesting that review the entire controversy surrounding the herb STEVIA. FDA's unconscionable withholding of this natural substance from the American people must be answered, once and for all.

Make good on DSHEA. Give STEVIA full legal status.

Yours truly,

Measurement Conversion Charts

Equivalent U.S. Standard, U.K. Imperial and Metric Measurements

In the United States we use standard measurement containers. Since the density of different ingredients varies, it is difficult to achieve accurate weight equivalents. For example, one cup of peanut butter weighs more than one cup of flour. Therefore, when converting standard American volume measurements, you should also measure volume, rather than weight. To make measuring even easier, American measuring cups and spoons are available in most major stores around the world.

Volume Conversions

Volume	U.S. Units	U.K. Units	Metric Units
1 teaspoon (US)	1/6 ounce	5/6 teaspoon	4.929 milliliters
1 tablespoon (US)	0.5 ounce	5/6 tablespoon	14.79 milliliters
1 fluid ounce (US)	1 ounce	1.041 ounces	29.57 milliliters
1 gill (US)	4 ounces	5/6 gill	118 milliliters
1 cup (US)	8 ounces	5/6 breakfast cup	236.6 milliliters
1 pint (US)	16 ounces	5/6 pint	473.2 milliliters
1 quart (US)	32 ounces	5/6 quart	946.3 milliliters
1 gallon (US)	128 ounces	5/6 gallon	3.785 liters
1 cubic inch	0.5541 ounces	0.5767 ounce	16.387 milliliters
1 teaspoon (UK)	1.2 teaspoons	0.2083 ounce	6.16 milliliters
1 dessert spoon (UK)	2.4 teaspoons	0.4167 ounce	12.32 milliliters
1 tablespoon (UK)	1.2 tablespoons	0.625 ounce	18.48 milliliters
1 fluid ounce (UK)	0.96076 ounces	1 ounce	28.4 milliliters
1 gill (UK)	1.2 gills	5 ounces	142 milliliters
1 breakfast cup (UK)	1.2 cups	10 ounces	284 milliliters
1 pint (UK)	1.2 pints	20 ounces	568 milliliters

Volume	U.S. Units	U.K. Units	Metric Units
1 quart (UK)	1.2 quarts	40 ounces	1.136 liters
1 gallon (UK)	1.2 gallons	160 ounces	4.546 liters
1 milliliter	0.203 teaspoon	0.169 teaspoon	1 milliliter
1 centiliter	2.03 teaspoons	1.69 teaspoons	10 milliliters
1 deciliter	0.423 cup	0.352 cup	100 milliliters
1 liter	1.057 quarts	0.8806 quart	1000 milliliters
1 decaliter	2.642 gallons	2.202 gallons	10000 milliliters
1 teaspoon (metric)	1.014 teaspoons	0.845 teaspoons	5 milliliters
1 tablespoon (metric)	3.04 tablespoons	2.54 tablespoons	15 milliliters
1 standard cup	1 cup	0.8806 cup	250 milliliters

Weight Conversions (Solid Measures)

Weight	U.K. / U.S. Units	Metric Units
1 ounce	1/16 pound	28.34952 grams
1 pound	16 ounces	453.592 grams
1 milligram	0.000035274 ounces	0.001 gram
1 centigram	0.00035274 ounces	0.01 gram
1 decigram	0.0035274 ounces	0.1 gram
1 gram	0.035274 ounces	1.0 gram
1 decagram	0.35274 ounces	10 grams
1 hectogram	3.5274 ounces	100 grams
1 kilogram	35.274 ounces	1000 grams
1 kilogram	2.204625 pounds	1000 grams

Length Conversions (Linear And Area Measures)

Length	U.K. / U.S. Units	Metric Units
1 inch	1/12 foot	2.54 centimeters
1 foot	12 inches	30.48 centimeters
1 yard	36 inches	91.44 centimeters
1 millimeter	0.03937 inches	0.1 centimeter
1 centimeter	0.3937 inches	1.0 centimeters
1 meter	39.37 inches	100 centimeters

Oven Temperature Equivalents

Fahrenheit	Celsius	Gas Mark	Description
225	110	1/4	Cool
250	130	1/2	
275	140	1	Very Slow
300	150	2	
325	170	3	Slow
350	180	4	
375	190	5	
400	200	6	Moderately Hot
425	220	7	Fairly Hot
450	230	8	Hot
475	240	9	Very Hot
500	250	10	Extremely Hot

Helpful Tips

Measurements

a pinch	$1/8$ teaspoon or less
3 teaspoons	1 tablespoon
4 tablespoons	$1/4$ cup
8 tablespoons	$1/2$ cup
12 tablespoons	$3/4$ cup
16 tablespoons	1 cup
2 cups	1 pint
4 cups	1 quart
4 quarts	1 gallon
8 quarts	1 peck
16 ounces	1 pound
32 ounces	1 quart
8 ounces liquid	1 cup
1 ounce liquid	2 tablespoons

(For liquid and dry measurements use standard measuring spoons and cups. All measurements are level.)

Substitutions

Ingredient	Quantity	Substitute
self rising flour	1 cup	1 cup all-purpose flour, $1/2$ tsp. salt, and 1 tsp. baking powder
cornstarch	1 tbsp.	2 tbsp. flour or 2 tsp. quick-cooking tapioca
baking powder	1 tsp.	$1/2$ tsp. baking soda plus $1/2$ tsp. cream of tartar
powdered sugar	1 cup	1 cup granulated sugar plus 1 tsp. corn-starch
brown sugar	$1/2$ cup	2 tbsp. molasses in $1/2$ cup granulated sugar
sour milk	1 cup	1 tbsp. lemon juice or vinegar plus sweet milk to make 1 cup (let stand 5 minutes)
whole milk	1 cup	$1/2$ cup evaporated milk plus $1/2$ cup water
cracker crumbs	$1/2$ cup	1 cup bread crumbs
chocolate	1 oz.	3 or 4 tbsp. cocoa plus 1 tbsp. butter*
fresh herbs	1 tbsp.	1 tsp. dried herbs
fresh onion	1 small	1 tbsp. instant minced onion, rehydrated
dry mustard	1 tsp.	1 tbsp. prepared mustard
tomato juice	1 cup	$1/2$ cup tomato sauce plus $1/2$ cup water
catsup	1 cup	1 cup tomato sauce plus $1/2$ cup sugar and 2 tbsp. vinegar
dates	1 lb.	$1 1/2$ cup dates, pitted and cut
bananas	3 medium	1 cup mashed
mini marshmallows	10	1 large marshmallow

*In substituting cocoa for chocolate in cakes, the amount of flour must be reduced.

Brown and white sugars: usually may be used interchangeably.

Vegetable Time Table

Vegetable	Cooking Method	Time
Asparagus	Boiled	10–15 minutes
Artichokes, French	Boiled	40 minutes
	Steamed	45–60 minutes
Beans, Lima	Boiled	20–40 minutes
	Steamed	60 minutes
Beans, String	Boiled	15–35 minutes
	Steamed	60 minutes
Beets, young with skin	Boiled	30 minutes
	Steamed	60 minutes
	Baked	70–90 minutes
Beets, old	Boiled or Steamed	1–2 hours
Broccoli, flowerets	Boiled	5–10 minutes
Broccoli, stems	Boiled	20–30 minutes
Brussel Sprouts	Boiled	20–30 minutes
Cabbage, chopped	Boiled	10–20 minutes
	Steamed	25 minutes
Cauliflower, stem down	Boiled	20–30 minutes
Cauliflower, flowerets	Boiled	8–10 minutes
Carrots, cut across	Boiled	8–10 minutes
	Steamed	40 minutes
Corn, green, tender	Boiled	5–10 minutes
	Steamed	15 minutes
	Baked	20 minutes
Corn on the cob	Boiled	8–10 minutes
	Steamed	15 minutes
Eggplant, whole	Boiled	30 minutes
	Steamed	40 minutes
	Baked	45 minutes
Parsnips	Boiled	25–40 minutes
	Steamed	60 minutes
	Baked	60–75 minutes
Peas, green	Boiled or Steamed	5–15 minutes
Potatoes	Boiled	20–40 minutes
	Steamed	60 minutes
	Baked	45–60 minutes
Pumpkin or Squash	Boiled	20–40 minutes
	Steamed	45 minutes
	Baked	60 minutes
Tomatoes	Boiled	5–15 minutes
Turnips	Boiled	25–40 minutes

References

Alverez, Mauro, "Contraceptive effect of the Stevia and of its sweetening principles", State University of Maringa, Dept. of Pharmacy and Pharmacology, Maringa, Brazil, October 1994.

Bonvie, Linda and Bill, and Gates, Donna, "The Stevia Story. A tale of incredible sweetness and intrigue" B.E.D. Publications, Atlanta, GA. p. 13 - 71.

Crammer, B., and R. Ikan. "Progress in the chemistry and properties of rebaudioside." Greenby, T.H., editor. Developments in Sweeteners. London, Elsevier, vol 3:45-64, 1987.

Ishii, Emy L.; Schwab, Andreas J.; Bracht, Adelar, "Inhibition of monosaccharide transport in the intact rat liver by stevioside". Departamento de Farmacia-Bioquimica, Universidade de Maringa; and Institut f.r Physiologische Chemie, Physikalische Biochemie und Zellbiologie der Universit‰t M.nchen. Printed in Biochemical Pharmacology, Vol. 36, No. 9, pp. 1417-1433, 1987.

Kerr, Warwick E., Mello, Maria Luiza S., and Bonadio, Evangelina, "Mutagenicity tests on the stevioside from Stevia rebaudiana (BERT.) Bertoni"

Kinghorn, A. Douglas, "Food Ingredient Safety Review: Stevia rebaudiana leaves", (March 16, 1992).

Kinghorn, A. D.; Soejarto, D. D.; Katz, N. L.; Kamath, S. K. "Studies to identify, idsolate, develop and test naturally occurring noncariogenic sweeteners that my be used as dietary sucrose substitutes." (Univ. Illinois, Chicago, Il. USA). Report 1983

Kleber, Carl J., "Rat dental caries investigation of stevioside natural sweetener", Purdue University, April 24, 1990.

Klongpanichpak, S., P. Temcharoen, C. Toskulkao, S. Apibal, and T. Glinsukon. "Lack of mutagenicity of stevioside and steviol in Salmonella typhimurium TA 98 and TA 100." Journal Medical Associations of Thailand, Sep; 80, Suppl 1:S121-128, 1997.

Matsui M., K. Matsui, Y. Kawasaki, Y. Oda, T. Noguchi, "Evaluation of the genotoxicity of stevioside and steviol using six in vitro and one in vivo mutagenicity assays." Mutagenesis, 11:573-579, 1996.

Nakayama, Kunio; Kasahara, Daigo; Yamamoto, Fumihiro, "Absorption, distribution, metabolism and excretion of Stevioside in Rats". Omiya Research Laboratory, Nikken Chemicals Co. Ltd.: 1-346, Kitabukuro-cho, Omiya, Saitama, Japan. March 1985

Nunes, P., and N.A. Pereira. "The effects of stevia rebaudiana on the fertility of experimental animals." Revista Brasileira de Farmacia, 69:46-50, 1988.

Pinheiro, Carlos Eduardo, "Effect of the Stevioside and of the aqueous extract of Stevia Rebaudiana (BERT) Bertoni on the glycemia of normal and diabetic rats", Presented to the II Brazilian Convention on Stevia rebaudiana (Bert) Bertoni - September 1982

Richard, David, "Stevia Rebaudiana, Nature's sweet secret". Vital Health Publishins, Bloomingdale, IL. p. 7 - 32.

"Stevia Rebaudiana: Description and Chemical Aspects", Inga S.A., Maringa, Brazil, 1989

Uehara, Olivia A.; Utino, Vivian H.; Miyata, Ivete; and Oliveira, Ricardo M. Filho, "Interaction of the stevioside with androgens" as presented to the 2nd Brazilian seminar on Stevia rebaudiana (BERT.) Bertoni. Dept. of Pharmacology, Institute of Medical Sciences, University of Sao Paulo.

Zhou, Ren; Ran, Zhijun; Li, Qiang; Zi, Xueli; Rong, Yingxin; Li, Renbiao, "Ion exchange methods in extraction and purification of steviosides from Stevia rebaudiana." Dep. Chem., Yunnan Norinal Univ., Peoples Republic of China. 1984

Stevia Internet References:

Aspartame Consumer Safety network
http://web2.airmail.net/marystod

Mission Possible (The largest source of aspartame information avalible.)
http://www.DORway.com

Herb Reasearch Foundation
http://www.herbs.org

Journalists Linda and Bill Bonvie
http://members.bellatlantic.net

Selected Aspartame References by H.J. Roberts, M.D., F.A.C.P.

Roberts, H.J.: Is aspartame (NutraSweet®) safe? On Call (official publication of the Palm Beach County Medical Society), 1987; January: 16-20.

Roberts, H.J.: Neurologic, psychiatric and behavioral reactions to aspartame in 505 aspartame reactions. In Proceedings of the First International Conference on Dietary Phenylalanine and Brain Function, edited by R.J. Wurtman and E. Ritter-Walker, Washington, D.C., 1987; May 8-10:477-481.

Roberts, H.J.: The Aspartame Problem. Statement for Committee on Labor and Human Resources, U.S. Senate, Hearing on "NutraSweet"-Health and Safety Concerns November 3, 1987. 83-178, U.S. Government Printing office, Washington, 1988:466-467.

Roberts, H.J.:Aspartame (Nutrasweet®) - associated confusion and memory loss: A possible human model for early Alzheimer's disease. Abstract 306. Annual meeting of the American Association for the advancement of Science, Boston, February 13, 1988.

Roberts, H.J.: Aspartame (Nutrasweet®) - associated epilepsy. Clinical Research 1988, 36:349A.

Roberts, H.J.: Complications associated with aspartame (Nutrasweet®) in diabetics. Clinical Research 1988; 3:489A.

Roberts, H.J.: Neurologic, psychiatric and behavioral reactions to aspartame in 505 aspartame reactions. In Proceedings of the First International Conference on Dietary Phenylalanine and Brain Function, edited by R.J. Wurtman and E. Ritter-Walker, Birkhauser, Boston, Inc., 1988, 373-376

Roberts, H.J.: Reactions attributed to aspartame-containing products: 551 cases. Journal of Applied Nutrition 1988; 40:85-94.

Roberts, H.J.: Adverse reactions to aspartame: Reply. Journal of Applied Nutrition 1989; 41:40-41.

Roberts, H.J.: Aspartame (Nutrasweet®): Is It Safe. Philadelphia, The Charles Press, 1989.

Roberts, H.J.: Is aspartame (Nutrasweet®) Safe? Public Health and Legal Challenges. In Proceedings for 30th Anniversary Conference on Legal Medicine. Orlando, Florida, March 15-17, 1990, 64-84.

Roberts, H.J.: Does aspartame cause human brain cancer? Journal of Advancement in Medicine 1991; 4 (Winter):231-241.

Roberts, H.J.: Aspartame-associated confusion and memory loss. Townsend Letter for Doctors 1991; June:442-443.

Roberts, H.J.: Aspartame, Is It Safe? Interview with H.J. Roberts, M.D. Mastering Food Allergies 1992; 7 (#1): 3-6.

Roberts, H.J.: Sweet'ner Dearest: Bittersweet Vignettes About Aspartame (Nutrasweet®). West Palm Beach, Sunshine Sentinel Press (P.O. Box 17799; ZIP 33416), 1992.

Roberts, H.J.: Unexplained headaches and seizures. Townsend Letter for Doctors 1992; November: 1001-1002.

Roberts, H.J.: Analysis of Adverse Reactions to Monosodium Glutamate. Testimony to Federation of American Societies for Experimental Biology, Bethesda. 1993; April 8.

Roberts, H.J.: Defense Against Alzheimer's Disease. West Palm Beach, Sunshine Sentinel Press, 1995.

Roberts, H.J.: Aspartame and headache. Neurology 1995; 45:1631-1633.

Roberts, H.J.: Professional Opinion Concerning the Use of Products Containing Aspartame (Nutrasweet®) by persons with diabetes and hypoglycemia, 1995.

Roberts, H.J.: Professional Opinion Concerning the Use of Products Containing aspartame (Nutrasweet®) by Pregnant women, infants and children, 1995.

Roberts, H.J.: Professional Opinion Concerning the Use of Products Containing aspartame (Nutrasweet®) by persons with eye problems, 1995.

Roberts, H.J.: Professional Opinion: Aspartame Disease Simulating Multiple Sclerosis, 1996.

Roberts, H.J.: Professional Opinion Concerning Cardiac and Chest Complaints Attributable to Products Containing aspartame (Nutrasweet®), 1996.

Roberts, H.J.: Aspartame and brain cancer. (Letter) The Lancet 1997; 349:362.

Roberts, H.J.: Preclinical Alzheimer's disease. (Letter) Neurology 1997; 48:549-550.

Roberts, H.J.: Aspartame and hyperthyroidism: A presidential affiliation reconsidered. Townsend Letter for Doctors & Patients May, 1997:86-88.

Roberts, H.J.: Professional Opinion Concerning Headaches Caused by the Use of Products Containing aspartame (Nutrasweet®), 1997.

Roberts, H.J.: Professional Opinion Concerning allergic reactions to Products Containing aspartame (Nutrasweet®), 1997.

Roberts, H.J.: Aspartame Effects During Pregnancy and Childhood. (Letter). Latitudes 1997; 3 (Number 1), p.3.

Roberts, H.J.: Critique of the Official Australia and New Zealand Food Authority (ANZFA) Position on Aspartame. Soil & Health 1997; July/September: p. 15.

Roberts, H.J.: Ignored Health Hazards for Pilots and Drivers. The A-B-C-D-E-F-G-H File. West Palm Beach, Sunshine Sentinel Press, 1998.

Roberts, H.J.: Submission to FDA regarding Docket No. 98F-0052 (Food Additive Petition for Neotame), March 3, 1998.

Roberts, H.J.: Breast Implants or Aspartame (Nutrasweet®) Disease? The Suppressed Opinion About a Perceived Medicolegal Travesty. West Palm Beach, Sunshine Sentinel Press, 1999.

Index

Q

R

S

V

vanilla,
    Vanilla Cream Cheese Frosting, 213
    Vanilla Cream Pie, 165
    Vanilla Ice Cream, 196
    Vanilla Ice Milk, 197
    Vanilla Pudding, 185
vegetables,
    Cinnamon Glazed Acorn Squash, 112
    German Red Cabbage, 88
    Gingered Vegetables, 107
    Harvest Time Beets, 109
    Maple Glazed Carrots, 109
    Maple Glazed Sweet Potatoes, 113
    Sweet Potato Casserole, 114
    Sweet-and Sour Carrots, 108
    Three-Bean Bake, 111
vegetarian main dishes,
    Balsamic Medallions, 127
    Chili, 128
    Dijon Tofu Salad, 94
    Pasta with Tofu, 132
    Seitan Cakes, 129
    Southwest Peppers, 130
    Spinach and Cheese Quiche, 131
    Sweet and Sour Vegetables, 108

W

Waffles,
    Cinnamon Nut Waffles, 77
    Banana Waffles, 77
Whipped Cream, 232
whipped toppings,
    Chocolate Whipped Cream, 232
    Light Whipped Topping, 231
    Whipped Cream, 231
White Sauce, 232
white-powdered stevia, 12, 22-23
whole leaf form, 3, 11, 19-22
Whole-wheat Applesauce Muffins, 55

Y

yeast bread, 41
yogurt,
    Fresh Fruit Yogurt, 195
    Orange Frozen Yogurt, 201
    Peachy Yogurt Shake, 66
    Piña Colada Frozen Yogurt, 202
    Pineapple-Peach Smoothie, 57
    Yogurt with Fruit Preserves, 194

Z

zucchini
    Buffalo Vegetables, 125
    Chili (Vegetarian), 128
    Zucchini or Apple Bread, 72

Other Books from Crystal Health Publishing

Low-Carb Cooking With Stevia:
The Naturally Sweet & Calorie-Free Herb

by James Kirkland

ISBN: 1-928906-14-1

The perfect companion for anyone on a low-carbohydrate eating plan! This book contains revolutionary, delicious recipes like pastas, breads, even cakes and cookies - all low in carbohydrates. Filled with practical advice, Mr. Kirkland is inspirational as he explains how he lost his extra weight and regained his life - All while enjoying a variety of favorite foods and never feeling hungry. Mr. Kirkland, an expert on stevia, includes in-depth information about stevia, the natural alternative to questionable artificial sweeteners. With over 175 revolutionary low-carb recipes and over 60 pages of important information, Low-Carb Cooking With Stevia is the essential companion for a successful low-carbohydrate lifestyle.

Sugar-Free Vegan Cooking With Stevia:
The Naturally Sweet & Calorie-Free Herb

By Tanya Kirkland & Gail Davis

AVAILABLE SPRING 2001

ISBN: 1-928906-16-8

Finally, a sugar-free cookbook that complements the healthy Vegan lifestyle. This inspirational cookbook is divided into two parts. The first part gives comprehensive information about the Vegan lifestyle and how to select and successfully use the sweet herb stevia. The second part contains easy to follow recipes that contain NO products derived from animals. Containing no dairy, eggs, sugar, or artificial sweeteners, plus numerous corn-free, soy-free, grain-free and gluten-free recipes, this remarkable cookbook is also perfect for those suffering from allergies. Best of all, over 100 recipes everyone will love.